9-14-19
Blessings!
Alice Wein Shiel

OLD
YELLOWED
HAT

OLD YELLOWED HAT

*and Other "Gems" to Bring
God Near to You*

BY
ALICE HEIN SCHIEL B.S., M.ED.

XULON PRESS ELITE

Xulon Press Elite
2301 Lucien Way #415
Maitland, FL 32751
407.339.4217
www.xulonpress.com

© 2018 by ALICE HEIN SCHIEL B.S., M.Ed.

All rights reserved solely by the author. The author guarantees all contents are original and do not infringe upon the legal rights of any other person or work. No part of this book may be reproduced in any form without the permission of the author. The views expressed in this book are not necessarily those of the publisher.

Unless otherwise indicated, Scripture quotations taken from the King James Version (KJV)–*public domain.*

Scripture quotations taken from the Amplified Bible (AMP). Copyright © 1954, 1958, 1962, 1964, 1965, 1987 by The Lockman Foundation. Used by permission. All rights reserved.

Printed in the United States of America.

ISBN-13: 978-1-54564-850-6

DEDICATION

This book is dedicated to my children Alyssa Hesketh, Billy Schiel, Byron Schiel, and Benjamin Schiel. You are truly my inspiration! It's also dedicated to Sara Callahan, a reader who told me she wanted to read my poetry. Thanks to Sara, this book includes poems written by yours truly.

Acknowledgements

Thanks to my husband Bill for encouraging me with this project and for help with proofreading. I appreciate the support at all of the book signings and speaking engagements with my first book (<u>Nora Mae, a Remarkable, Insignificant Person</u>) and my heart is filled with gratitude for helping me get book number two accomplished!

Thanks to my sister Sarah Muñoz who did the majority of the proofreading of the manuscript. It would not have looked quite so polished without her help! Thanks for the encouragement and for allowing me to include one of your writings. It appears on pages 74, 75.

Thanks to my mother-in-law Hazel Schiel for the "**gems**" she recorded over the years and passed along to me. They are the heart of this work.

Special thanks to my good friends Deb Dousay and Debbie Carter who were faithful to prod me with, "How is the book coming? I can't wait to read it!" Thanks for believing in me!

Contents

Poems and Drawings

Walk With Me	1
Encounter at Richard and Lynda's River Place	11
Drawing–Hat	16
Old Yellowed Hat	17
Me, the Candle	23
Humility	28
Blind	33
Hunter's Anticipation	39
New Horizons For an Old Girl	44
I.C.U.	51
Vandal in the Night	57
Slandered	63
Little Chick-a-dee	68
Christmas Thoughts	74
Amazing!	80
Barbara Bush	87
Sleepy Morning	94
Pretty Girl	101
Message	106
Sounds of the Rain	113
Stretching	119
My Shepherd	124
Drawing – Shepherd	125
I Can't Live in the Valley	130
Maturing	133

Introduction

Old Yellowed Hat is a book of poems and short devotionals to help you, the reader, focus on God daily. In our busy lives we sometimes find our moments with God being crowded out. This book is set-up for you to read one page a day, Monday through Friday, and ponder the message: laugh, cry, or merely think as you allow God to speak to you. Start your week with a poem on Monday, followed by uplifting devotionals for Tuesday through Friday. Saturday and Sunday are left open for your week-end church studies.

Many things can trigger happy memories for us. One day I took my daddy's old straw hat from the closet shelf that has been its home since he died, more than forty years ago. At once it seemed my dad was with me; I could see his smile, hear his laugh. I wrote a poem to capture the memory. The writings in this book are a gift from God, our Heavenly Father. As the old hat brought my daddy near, these writings are meant to bring God close to you. Listen to what He is saying; gain strength to face your day's challenges. God loves you. Enjoy being with Him, share his message with a friend or two.

When I moved to Houston, Texas in 1971 I chose to travel to Decker Prairie which was twenty miles north of Houston to attend church. I was a high school graduate enrolled in Midwest Bible Institute. At Deckers Chapel

I met a lady named Hazel Schiel. Two years later when I married her son, Bill, she became my mother-in-law. Mom Schiel was what I called her. She was an avid reader and kept notebooks of interesting sayings she found, heard in sermons, or copied from church signs. Years later she gave those notebooks to Bill and me.

Old Yellowed Hat is a gathering of my poetry and short devotionals I have written based on "**gems**" from Mom Schiel's notebooks. I want you to find God's presence as you pause from your busy schedule, read, and listen.......

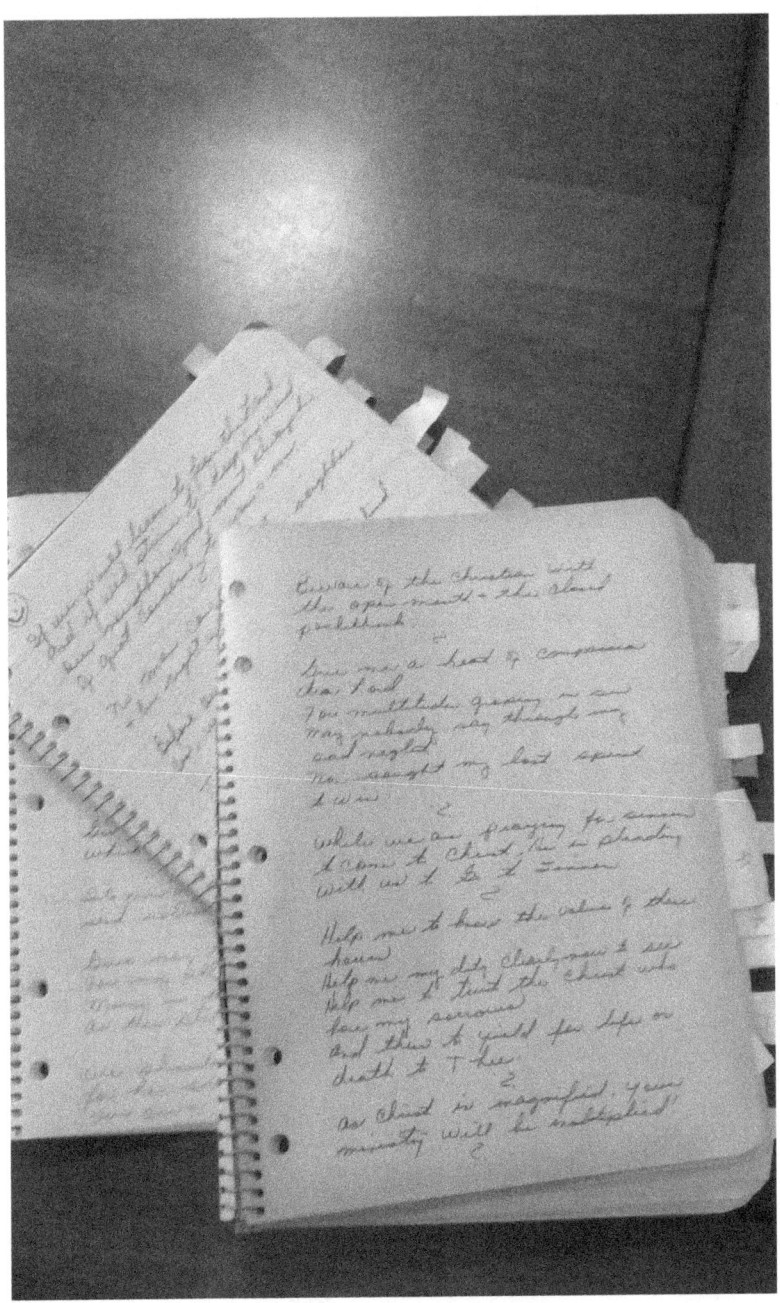

Mom Schiel's notebooks

Now before us zinn'as be

Walk With Me!

My friend, come walk beside me
Hearts singing as we go
Color you have got to see
Beyond the weeds that grow!

Remember days of childhood
Catch the carefree "air" we felt
Step or dance as once we could
For now our troubles melt.

"**Orange!**" shouts the first flower
Bold, bright, thirteen petals,
Center screams, "Pollen power"
Grown-ups feel this nettle-

Not us! For this stroll, we're kids
Our eyes still full of wonder,
Locked on magnificent **red**
Blooms; we gasp, stare, and ponder.

Now before us zinn'as be
Their blooms four inches wide
Tossed by wind, so happily
Swaying from side to side.

"More than one hundred petals
On my shoot!" **purple** one cries,
"Try to top that if you can."
Stunning **yellow** blossom sighs,

"We each have unique beauty.
The bees adorn my crown."
Miss **Pink** just nods to agree.
A bee floats to the ground.

Alice Hein Schiel B.S., M.Ed.

Walk With Me!
Cont'd

Ten butterflies flit about
Bees dance and sing with a beat.
"Pollen sacks are full!" they shout,
"We are wobbling on our feet!"

Tall sunflowers bow their heads.
Sunlight has us baptized
As it covers all these beds
Like glitter synchronized.

We're mesmerized by this show
And time does seem to hurry.
Palates do not want to go.
We've tasted nature's curry.

(You are starting on a wonderful journey. Walk with me. Allow God to speak to you daily as you taste His heavenly curry.)

Alice Hein Schiel

Now before us zinn'as be

Hazel's Gem #1:
"You'll go forth a little stronger, with a fresh supply of grace
If each day you meet the Savior in a secret, quiet place."

Good morning! (or Good evening if you find your quiet place at the end of your day!) The Psalmist David wrote, "I will lift up mine eyes unto the hills, from whence cometh my help. My help cometh from the LORD, which made heaven and earth." "The Lord is thy keeper: the LORD is thy shade upon thy right hand. The sun shall not smite thee by day, nor the moon by night. The LORD shall preserve thee from all evil: he shall preserve thy soul." Psalms 121: 1,2,5-7.

Look again at verse six. David says, "The sun shall not smite thee by day, nor the moon by night." Whatever the stresses are that you will face, or have faced, this day they will not overwhelm you; they will not defeat you! Why? Because the LORD shall preserve you. When David was a shepherd the sun's heat could sometimes seem unbearable. When people traveled the sun would drain their energy as they walked. If they rode animals, the animals would also be affected by the heat. Whatever your stresses are this day, God promises that they will not "smite" you! That is so good to know when reports are due and the criteria is changed by someone who is "making things easier" for you. When people are upset with you (with or without reason) the LORD will preserve you! If your job requires long hours into the night or if you have the night shift, the moon will not "smite you" by night! You are in good hands.

Alice Hein Schiel B.S., M.Ed.

Hazel's Gem #2:
> "I expect to pass this world but once
> Therefore if there be any kindness I can show
> or any good thing I can do to any fellow
> human being, let me not defer or neglect it,
> for I shall not pass this way again."

Arise and greet the world with a smile or a song, whichever you can generate! If the rain is falling outside or in your heart, receive it as God's gift to water the seeds planted. The trees, the flowers in our world produce seeds that must be watered or they will not grow. God has placed a seed of greatness within YOU. It, too, must be watered or it cannot grow. Be aware of God's presence today and look for an opportunity to show kindness to another: open a door when someone's hands are full; greet your co-workers with a "good morning"; if you tied at the 3-way stop, let someone else go first; help an older person put groceries in their car and then park the grocery cart for them; wash, dry, fold, and put away your spouse's socks (they will not be able to find them, and may faint when they do, but they will feel loved!).

Hazel's Gem #3:
> "You teach a little bit by what you say, but you teach most by what you are."

Hazel's Gem #4:
> "I used to censor everyone
> I was a Pharisee
> Until quite unexpectedly
> I got a glimpse of me."

Hazel's gem reminds us to to be less judgmental of others. In the scripture Jesus challenges us with these words:

"Judge not, that ye be not judged.

"For with what judgment ye judge, ye shall be judged: and with what measure ye mete, it shall be measured to you again.

"And why beholdest thou the mote that is in thy brother's eye, but considerest not the beam that is in thine own eye?" Matt. 7:1-3 (KJV)

You should routinely examine yourself and confess your faults to God. Holy Communion time at church is a good time to do this. However, if you see a "beam in your eye" today – get it out! Once you see the fault and confess it, let it go. Receive His forgiveness and continue on. You are cleansed! Your garment is white! There is no room for guilt – let it go. Jesus has washed the sin away.

Today is a good day to laugh at yourself. Enjoy the people or person God places along your pathway. It will be fun to see who it is. Be ready to smile.

Alice Hein Schiel B.S., M.Ed.

Hazel's Gem #5:
> "His grace is sufficient, thou ne'er canst exhaust it.
> Be strong in the grace which floweth to thee.
> Draw largely, continually out of His fullness.
> Thy strength and thy shield He ever will be."

Wow! Now that's some "King James" English! I hope you can grasp the meaning. You can "ne'er" exhaust it (ne'er is "never"; the poet probably left out the v to have one syllable in the word, instead of two). Grace will never run out. God has more than you need. The strength you need for this day is available, but you have to tap into it. To "draw out" means to take out or extract what you need from God's supply. His river is flowing. If you need love, take some. If you need joy, He's got it; if you need peace, it awaits; if you need self-control, it's there for you; if you need His protection, it is available. You can extract it by acknowledging Him in prayer.

"In the day when I cried thou answeredst me, and strengthenedst (don't you love beautiful English) me with strength in my soul.

"Though I walk in the midst of trouble, thou wilt revive me: thou shalt stretch forth thine hand against the wrath of mine enemies, and thy right hand shall save me." Psalms 138: 3, 7 KJV

"Though I walk in the midst of trouble, thou wilt revive me"

Dancin' River Ranch

Encounter at Richard and Lynda's River Place

I see it all around me.
I hear it as the wind whispers through the leaves.
I sense God's love as a bee
Lands on the table and sits beyond my sleeve.

> The choir of birds sings aloud.
> A hummingbird wins first rights to the water,
> Then waits, enjoying the cloud
> Cover; pink bumps the sky and nightfall totters.

A fawn emerges, skipping near its mother.
Fireflies dart above the knoll.
The message comes in one way, then another.
An axis bark stirs my soul.

> Alice! God loves you! God loves you! God loves you!
> Creation is crying out –
> A brief silence affirms God's presence anew.
> Listen! You will hear Him shout……..

Alice Hein Schiel

Hazel's Gem #6:

"Though there are dangers untold and stern confronting me in the way,
willingly still would I go, not turn –
But trust Thee for grace each day."

Amazing God! He woke you up this morning! He has plans for you today! Whatever challenges you face today, God faces them with you. In Psalms 91 (KJV) verses 11-13, the psalmist declares,

"For he shall give his angels charge over thee, to keep thee in all thy ways.

"They shall bear thee up in their hands, lest thou dash thy foot against a stone.

"Thou shalt tread upon the lion and adder: the young lion and the dragon shalt thou trample under feet."

Look for places today to trust God. Mentally cast your care upon Him. Choose to take one step at a time in the right direction. I remember as a child collecting eggs, when I ran from the chickens, they got boisterous, flapped their wings and chased me as I ran toward the gate with my heart pounding. I was frightened this way many times. I finally discovered that if I collected the eggs and got enough boldness to walk away (instead of running), the chickens would walk with me or they would step away from me.

If you can convince your heart to trust God, his grace will help you through unpredictable stress mines. He may even defuse them for you!

Hazel's Gems #7:

"Just when I need Him Jesus is near
Just when I falter, Just when I fear
Ready to help me, ready to cheer
Just when I need Him most."

#8:

"The quickest way to get back on your feet is to get down on your knees."

A wonderful day this is! It is wonderful because of who our Creator is. If we honor Him and walk in His ways, the great God (Jehovah, El Shaddi, Jehovah- jireh) will intervene for us.

No matter how you got knocked down the way to gain the strength to stand again is through prayer. Getting down on your knees is a picture of your spirit bowing to God. It shows humility. Admitting failure or brokenness is the first step to recovery. If someone has knocked you down, getting down on your knees symbolizes that you give up your inner desire "to be right" or "to get back at them." It depicts you giving the situation to God and letting him give you strength to be humiliated without bitterness or grudges, and strength to stand again, unashamed.

"Vengeance is mine; I will repay, saith the Lord." Romans 12:19b

"Be not overcome of evil, but overcome evil with good." Romans 12: 21

God is so much more powerful than evil. Another thing – if you have a long drive to work, you can pray while you drive. Do not close your eyes, of course! Let your spirit bow down; drop to your knees later.

Alice Hein Schiel B.S., M.Ed.

Hazel's Gem #9:
> "Children close their ears to advice but open their eyes to Example."

Do you encounter children in your normal daily routine? Look for children this day. Be aware that small eyes follow you. May they see the fruit of the spirit hanging from your boughs. Think of yourself as a tree with all this beautiful fruit attached: love, joy, peace, longsuffering, gentleness, goodness, meekness, temperance, and faith (listed in Galatians 5:22, 23). You are giving them food for today, and also a seed that will produce these same virtues as their personalities develop. Media bombards them with all the wrong things: adultery, fornication, uncleanness, lasciviousness, idolatry, witchcraft, hatred, variance, emulations, wrath, strife, seditions, heresies, envyings, murders, drunkenness, and revellings. Galatians 5:21 tells us that those who "do such things shall not inherit the kingdom of God."

I remember my children singing with the same accent as their Sunday School teacher, setting the table just as I did, and eating Blue Bell ice cream from the carton like their dad. May the little eyes that glance your way today find **good** fruit.

Hazel's Gem # 10:
"No service in itself is small;
None great though Earth it fill;
But that is small that seeks its own
And great that seeks God's will."

Hazel's Diamond:
"Today's mighty oak is just yesterday's little nut
That held its ground."

Don't give up! Despise not the day of small things! Be faithful where you are with what you have. These words are fertilizer for your spirit. No matter where you are on your journey, with need or with giant storehouses, there is always someone more wealthy, someone smarter, and someone more successful than you. You must not get trapped into measuring yourself by another's abilities. Take advantage of the opportunities God places before you today. You can't offer great knowledge if you have little. But you can use what you have and God will bless it. It's funny how He multiplies our gifts if we do not hoard them. He multiplies our finances as we give away what He instructs us to give.

You may be at a place where all you can give is a bit of time or a flower from your garden, but there is someone who needs that. On this big planet, you are making a difference.

"…I will bless you…and you will be a blessing." Genesis 12:2 (Amplified Bible)

Old Yellowed Hat

Alice Hein Schiel

It's just an old yellowed hat
Been on my closet shelf for years
A once fine, but now bent straw hat
Somehow it brings my Daddy near.

He died when I was still a teen
Embarking on my life's fresh dreams.
A treasure made of straw that's flat,
I'm glad I saved my Daddy's hat.

Silly, forty-five-year-old hat
My head's too small or it's too fat
The mem'ries bounce and just like that:
I hear him laugh; I see him smile
I indulge myself a short while.

Sweet mem'ries that were tucked away
Flood my heart and mind this day.
I smile and then I shed a tear…
This yellowed hat from Daddy dear.

(my Daddy, **Hugo Hein**, was born July 14, 1905; died April 28, 1972)

Hazel's Gem # 11:
> "Don't expect a million dollar answer to a single 10-cent prayer."

I can envision prayer warrior Hazel quoting this one! Her love for humor was so delightful and one of the reasons people enjoyed being around her. We want to call on God at our leisure, state our need, and hurry on to the next thing. It's the time acknowledging God's presence before you ask or time spent reading the **Bible** that adds value to your prayer. God wants to be more than your 9-1-1 call when in distress. He wants to walk with you every day.

"But if I pray about something more than once that means I lack faith." Not true! There are times when you must pray more than once.

Luke 11:10 (Amplified Bible) "For everyone who asks and keeps on asking receives; and he who seeks and keeps on seeking finds; and to him who knocks and keeps on knocking, the door shall be opened."

PS. If I didn't honor God in my life and I desperately needed Him, I would try my 10-cent prayer. He is merciful! Then I would change my habits to include Him in my routine every day.

Hazel's Gem # 12:
"The bore chatters on
Never losing his breath.
His way to kill time
Is to talk it to death"

The two boys sat on a lonely fishing pier at a quiet lake. Both were relaxing, enjoying the warm sunshine and cool breeze. The first boy expounded on his dreams; he built castles with his words, climbed mountains, and charged enemies. "Someday I will sail the ocean!" His friend listened quietly, drawn in by the descriptive enthusiasm pouring forth.

He said, "I want to sail the ocean too! I will…"

The first boy never heard his friend but continued to describe his own visions. He stared at the sky, watching the cloud formations. "I will sail to many ports and meet strange and interesting people. I will see the green hills of Ireland and meet the men with fiery tempers!"

The friend said, "I want to sail to Australia…"

The first boy never heard him. He continued to describe his own illusions. "I shall meet the Queen of England and receive her knightship…" He looked around; his friend was gone.

I Corinthians 13:1 "Though I speak with the tongue of men and of angels and have not charity, I am become as sounding brass, or a tinkling cymbal."

Hazel's Gem # 13:
"People who speak volumes usually end up on the shelf."

Alice Hein Schiel B.S., M.Ed.

Hazel's Gem # 14:
> "O give us homes where Christ is Lord and master,
> The Bible read, the precious hymns still sung –
> Where prayer comes first in peace or in disaster
> And praise is natural speech to every tongue."

Today I think of family heritage. Our homes reflect what we are. A woman's home reflects her spirit. If you want to have peace and joy felt in your dwelling continue to think on God daily and read the Bible regularly; even one verse is powerful. The fact that you are using this devotional shows that you are giving time to allow your spirit to tap into God's provision for today.

Make it your goal to pray and to read this manual every day, but don't beat yourself up if you fail. Simply jump back in, don't quit. Once you begin reaping peace and joy in your home you will make sure you are tapping into the source. God's word and a prayer when you are doing well will exercise your spirit so that you are confidently able to walk through any trial life brings.

Psalms 121:1, 2a (KJV) "I will lift up mine eyes unto the hills, from whence cometh my help. My help cometh from the Lord…"

Hazel's Gem # 15:
"Lord, put a seal upon my lips.
Help me to guard with care
The things I say and swift repeat.
O' tongue of mine, beware!"

 # 16:
"Lots of things are opened by mistake,
But none so often as the mouth."

It's a good idea to be careful what you say, particularly when your emotions are involved. Love, anger, jealousy, hate, and exuberance bring out overzealous conversation. I have heard it said that words are like a bunch of feathers emptied on a breeze. Once released, it is impossible to ever get them all back. Train yourself to pause and count to ten before responding to hurtful comments. (Give your brain a chance to kick in before you respond!)

During casual conversation one can be tempted to express things about other people that are better left unsaid. We turn gossip into a "prayer request" so we can pass it on without feeling guilty. There are many scriptures about our words. Words, spoken or written, have power to create and power to tear down. Sometimes we have to address situations. Remember to do it with kindness.

Psalms 19:14 (KJV): "Let the words of my mouth and the meditation of my heart, be acceptable in thy sight, O Lord, my strength and my redeemer."

Shine Brightly

Me, the Candle

I sit here in the "quiet," waiting
All alone, but not really alone.
The birds sing loudly as they
  Frequent feeders outside my window.

The deer saunter by, looking for corn
A myriad of feelings washes over me:
Earlier one Facebook friend posted
  Photos of her Ireland trip;

Another friend posts, "My son has drowned;"
One rejoices that her new, preemie,
Twin grandsons are doing well.
Another friend's sister died today…

"Rejoice with those who rejoice,
  Weep with those who weep," the <u>Bible</u> says.
This tapestry called "life" does
  Sometimes take my breath away.

In the face of confusion
A calmness envelopes me.
"Ye are the light of the world."
"Shine brightly," I say to myself.

Alice Hein Schiel

Hazel's Gem # 17:
"I am my neighbor's <u>Bible</u>, he reads me when we meet.
Today he reads me in my home, tomorrow on the street.
He may be relative or friend – or slight acquaintance be.
He may not even know my name, yet he is reading me."

Are you a "Good morning, Lord!" or a "Good Lord, it's morning" kind of guy? Not sure?

Your neighbor can answer this question about you. Who are your neighbors? Perhaps it's your spouse, your children, drivers in your part of the traffic flow, the attendant at the drive-through window, your coworkers; on and on the list goes. They are all reading you. What kind of message are they getting? It may not be natural for you to be bubbly in the morning, but you can show kindness and goodness. Be polite, be civil, be caring.

Your sphere of influence increases as your day progresses. You are the only <u>Bible</u> that some folks will read today. As you let the fruit of the Spirit flow through you, your life becomes a clearer portrait of Jesus.

"…you yourselves are our letter of recommendation (our credentials), written in your hearts, to be known (perceived, recognized) and **read** by everybody."

II Corinthians 3:2 (Amplified Bible)

Hazel's Gem #18:
"Never let a bleak past becloud a bright future."

Now, what in the world does "becloud" mean? I could have guessed, but I wanted to be sure so I went to the dictionary. Becloud means to cloud over, to obscure, which is to darken or make dim.

God's promises are not contingent on your past. Even yesterday is a part of the past. Your future starts now! Every experience you have encountered can be used by God to give you understanding and ability to help someone else. Trust him and his promise to believers. When you begin to walk on God's path He gives you a brand new map. When you detour along the way, He forgives and guides you back to his path if you ask Him. Your future is bright because you walk with the King of Kings and Lord of Lords! This day will be bright, not because there are no challenges – but because you don't face challenges alone. When you continue to walk on God's path, He will take you places you never dreamed possible. You will see miracles you never envisioned.

Psalms 23:6 (KJV) – "Surely goodness and mercy shall follow me all the days of my life: and I will dwell in the house of the Lord forever."

Hazel's Gems # 19:
"If your religion won't take you to church.
How will it get you to Heaven?"

20:
"The church needs more love and less "lip,"
More action and less faction."

21:
"Many people use religion like a bus-
They ride it only when it is going their way."

There's something supernatural about committing to meet with other believers. It can be scary to think about sharing the joys and burdens of other people and even scarier to think about trusting them with your life. Being committed to other believers will strengthen you in every part of your life. You may graduate from school and retire from your job, but you never outgrow attending church. Mainly because we don't just attend church, we are the church.

You may think that by staying home on Sunday you save time and don't have to exhibit as much of the fruit of the Spirit because you have fewer folks to put up with, and certainly fewer hypocrites to rise above. However, when you give time to Him, God has a way of multiplying your time. Let someone try your fruit; you don't want it to get stale.

God's presence is with you in a greater way today because you gathered with His church on Sunday.

"Not forsaking the assembling of ourselves together..."
Hebrews 10:25a (KJV)

Hazel's Gem # 22:
"Blessings, yes we have so many
We could never name them all;
So let's lift our hearts in gladness
For God's favors great and small."

Psalms 103: 1-5 (KJV)
"Bless the Lord, O my soul: and all that is within me, bless his holy name.

"Bless the Lord, O my soul, and forget not all his benefits:

"Who forgiveth all thine iniquities; who healeth all thy diseases;

"Who redeemeth thy life from destruction; who crowneth thee with <u>lovingkindness</u> and tender mercies;

"Who satisfieth thy mouth with good things; so that thy youth is renewed like the eagle's."

The psalmist David gave us a beautiful list of God's blessings. These blessings are yours, they are for everyone. But you also have a personal list of blessings that you should thank God for. Say them aloud today. Let God know you are grateful. The scripture says that God dwells in the praises of His people. As you thank Him, you will sense more of His presence with you.

Lift your heart "in gladness." David's list actually goes on and on. Once you start yours, it will go on and on also. I'm going to start my list today by thanking God for the beautiful wild flowers I saw in the woods. What is your first thing?

Alice Hein Schiel B.S., M.Ed.

Humility

What a day this is – mark it down!
Decision made, face will not frown.
Brush aside intended potions,
And address the silly notions.

Never gonna' get me down, No –
Slide off my back; I tell you, "Go"
I'm pushing aside despair, tears
"Spirit of control, flee from here."

So I decide to rise; I'll fly!
The Holy Spirit lifts me high.
I know I have good qualities –
Quite a few; I will bend my knees.

With thankful heart, I laugh aloud.
God, you are good; I won't be proud.
I'll glean and learn. To pass this test,
I'm all ears, God, I will be blessed.

I'll learn more than I knew before.
"Quiet, self. Mind, open your door
And let another 'show you up.'
You do not know it all, old pup!"

Alice Hein Schiel

Hazel's Gems # 23:
>"I've found a little remedy
>To ease the life we live
>And make each day a happier one;
>It is the word "Forgive.""

 # 24:
>"He who cannot forgive others
>Breaks the bridge over which he
>Himself must pass."

 # 25:
>"Temper is what gets most of us in trouble.
>Pride is what keeps us there."

Jesus gives us the key to forgiveness in Matt. 6: 14 and 15 (KJV). Why is it so important? "For if ye forgive men their trespasses, your heavenly Father will also forgive you:

"But if ye forgive not men their trespasses, neither will your Father forgive your trespasses."

We are human, therefore we are not perfect and need God to forgive us. When we become a part of God's kingdom we must take on the attributes of our heavenly Father. We forgive others and then when we make a mistake He readily forgives us.

As you "walk through today" keep this in mind. You may need to forgive the person who darts in front of you as you drive to work; it may be the coworker who gossips about you; you may have a deep wound caused by someone's maliciousness aimed at you. Determine to forgive, asking God to help you. He will.

Hazel's Gems # 26:
"Prayerless pews make for powerless pulpits."

 # 27: "4 Ways to get rid of your preacher:
1) Look him straight in the eye while he is preaching and say "Amen" once in a while – He'll preach himself to death.
2) Pat him on the back and tell him his good points; before you know it, he'll work himself to death.
3) Rededicate your own life to Christ and ask your minister for a job to do; he'll die of heart failure.
4) Get the church to unite in prayer for him, and he'll soon become so effective that a larger congregation will take him off your hands."

I hope you enjoyed a chuckle or a laugh as you were reading. Laughter is good for you! Proverbs 17:22 (KJV) – "a merry heart doeth good like a medicine: but a broken spirit drieth the bones." Wow! Laughter brings health, even to our bones. The center of the bone is where the bone marrow is and the bone marrow contains our very life, our blood. Laughter even makes you look better. If you smile often, you get fewer wrinkles than if you frown often. (Smiling uses less muscles than frowning!)

So, today find ways to smile, even laugh! Be aglow for God.

Hazel's Gem # 28:
> "Trust Him when dark doubts assail thee
> Trust Him when thy strength is small
> Trust Him when to simply trust Him
> Seems the hardest thing of all."

What a blessing to have another day to walk on this earth! What a blessing to have a Savior to hold your hand when the ideas flung at you seem so topsy turvy! What a blessing to have His word to guide you and keep your focus clear!

"Thy word is a lamp unto my feet, and a light unto my path." Psalm 119:105 (KJV)

Our lives are full of choices and some are not easy to make, but God can give you peace in your decisions. Some decisions are very clear, He will not lead you against His word. At other times we have to make our best choice. Do I change jobs? Should I move to another city? Do I buy this car? Follow your goals and keep peace in your heart.

You may need to turn off the loud noise bombarding you, be it media or negative people. Hear His still small voice. Look for God's light and follow it.

"And whosoever of you will be the chiefest, shall be servant of all.

"For even the Son of man came not to be ministered unto, but to minister…"

Mark 10: 44, 45 (KJV)

Hazel's Gem # 29:
"Be careful what you say, dear friends
For many errors have occurred
When 'pseudo experts' aired their views
As if they were God's creative word."

 # 30:
"Many who won't talk with a full mouth
Will talk with an empty head."

Don't be guilty! Watch those words. The book of James admonishes us to "be swift to hear, slow to speak, slow to wrath." (James 1:19 KJV)

James 3:6 – "And the tongue is a fire, a world of iniquity: so is the tongue among our members, that it defileth the whole body, and setteth on fire the course of nature; and it is set on fire of hell."

James 3:2 "For in many things we offend all. If any man offend not in word, the same is a perfect man, able to bridle the whole body."

Think before you speak. When anger wells up inside of you, it is sometimes beneficial to count to ten before you speak. Give yourself a chance to form an acceptable response.

Choosing your words is something you will work on forever it seems. There are always opportunities to let it slip. Don't be too proud to say, "I'm sorry," when you need to. Put out the fire!

Blind

Alice Hein Schiel

I want to write a poem today.
I want to write it down.
The inspiration will not come.
I feel a silly frown.

I want to write a poem today.
I've said it at least twice.
I will be careful with my words.
I promise to write "nice."

O inspiration, come to me
And bring bold words to say.
Please let me write a poem this hour.
Help me to find a way.

So many voices in our world.
The words seem like clatter.
I want my message to ring out,
All this fog to shatter!

But inspiration will not come.
I guess no rhyme today.
I just wonder how I missed it-
No poem will come my way.

(Don't overlook the door God opens for you today.
Recognize your opportunity.)

Hazel's Gem # 31:
> "Yes, all of life takes on a different **hue**
> when we spend our time counting our blessings
> rather than airing our complaints.
> Don't be an ungrateful grumbler!"

When I hear the word "hue" I think of all the beautiful wild flowers we see in Texas most of the year. In spring the shades of color are gorgeous! When driving, a patch of gray turns to blue if the sun comes out from behind the clouds. That's the way our complaints work: they make life seem a dingy gray. But when the complaints are gone, the beautiful things can be seen clearly.

When we are thankful it opens our eyes to the beauty around us. The groceries that were "so heavy to carry in" become "the bounty God has supplied for our table!" The "long line we waited in for hours" becomes "an opportunity to chat with someone new." "You clumsy goof! You broke my salad bowl" becomes "It's okay. I'm amazed that wedding present lasted this long! We enjoyed it forty-two years!"

I Thessalonians 5:18 – "In everything give thanks for this is the will of God in Christ Jesus concerning you." We don't have to be thankful <u>for</u> everything, but <u>in</u> every situation we are to be thankful. Life will be brighter.

Hazel's Gem # 32:
"When fear knocks at the door, send faith to open it and you'll find no one there."

Fear comes in all sorts of packages, but faith trounces every one of them. A phobia is the irrational fear or dread of a particular thing or situation. The list of named phobias is pages long; faith trumps every one.

There are a few healthy fears. We are instructed to "fear God" in I Peter 2:17. This fear is a holy respect. A fear of heights may keep a child from injuring himself. A fear of water can keep a nonswimmer from danger.

I John chapter 4 tells you that God loves you and that love casts "out fear: because fear hath torment." As you grow in your Christian walk your faith becomes stronger. When fear tries to torment you remind yourself that God is in control. As His child you can have confidence that He will help you through every situation. "For God hath not given us the spirit of fear; but of power, and of love, and of a sound mind." II Timothy 1:7 (KJV)

I'm not saying you should ride over Niagara Falls in a barrel, but should you find yourself in a waterfall of fear God will give you the ideas you need to safely escape.

Alice Hein Schiel B.S., M.Ed.

Hazel's Gem # 33:
> "Nothing is hid from His all-seeing eye
> Never a teardrop nor ever a sigh.
> Anxious and troubled you never need be
> Trust Him completely and dark things will flee."

Your journey on Earth is full of variety. You will have days of sunshine and days filled with rain. Perhaps the storm clouds and wind threaten to blow you away. Tell God your feelings, admit that you need wisdom or strength. Confess your faults. One thing is sure – you can never change other people. The only person you can change is yourself. You can change how you react to other people, but only God can change them – when they allow Him to. Pray for them, yes. More importantly, ask God to show you how you can react or how you can deal with the bad situation. Trust Him and know that He is beside you. There is an old song which says,

"His eye is on the sparrow, I know He watches me."

Think of the birds; God supplies their every need. They sing rain or shine.

Matthew 10:29, 31 (KJV) – "Are not two sparrows sold for a farthing? And one of them shall not fall on the ground without your Father."

"Fear ye not therefore, ye are of more value than many sparrows."

Hazel's Gem # 34:
"He who is 'born of God' should
Increasingly resemble his Father."

Hazel's Gem # 35:
"It is not the sense of His presence,
But the fact of His presence that is our strength."

Dr. Bill Stephens of Merced, California recorded a series of teachings on "Who We Are in Christ." The greatness that Jesus manifested is planted in you. It is good to remind yourself who you belong to. Look in the mirror – God's Word. Are you looking more like Jesus? His love and kindness were unparalleled. He trusted the Father when it led to the cross. He edified those around him, yet resisted the complainers and hypocrites. He influenced all. You will influence everyone you meet today. Will they be glad you are a part of their day or will they say, "Here comes ol' grumpy! Run for cover"?

It has been said that a smile attracts a smile, and a good compliment lasts for 30 days; those are two easy ways to reflect kindness. God is love; God is life; and God is light. People can feel energized by your demeanor. They can see the right path by watching you. They will form an opinion of God by seeing His kid – You!

II Cor. 6:18 (KJV) – "And will be a Father unto you, and ye shall be my sons and daughters…"

Mel B

Hunter's Anticipation

*If I could shoot an axis
How happy I would be
Icing on a choc'late cake!
Winning the lottery!
*Four and one half months I've planned
And worked in cool and heat
I've built deer stand and feeders
And dreamed of this great feat!
*I've read about his habits
I've googled many sites
My magazines display the pics
I dream as smiles alight.
*If I could shoot an axis
How happy I would be
Wouldn't even mind the work
I'd clean him, happily
*I've watered all the grasses
Bought corn and sweet feed too
My cam'ras boast his picture
His bugle is not new
*I hear him in the evening
He's right across the knoll
If I could shoot that axis-
Sweet blessing for my soul!
*My bow and string are perfect
The arrow waits with glee
I'm ready, oh, so ready
To harvest – old Mel B.

(Mel B is a name fondly given to an axis deer that we saw several times. He was very thickly built. Bill's brother Richard named him for Mel Blount who was a linebacker for the Pittsburgh Steelers.)

Alice Hein Schiel

Alice Hein Schiel B.S., M.Ed.

Hazel's Gem # 36:
"The Lord's hand has painted the rainbow
You see His design in all things
When looking for wisdom, you'll find it
In stars, birds, and butterfly wings."

Good grief! The world is beautiful! The hand of God is never more seen than in the colors of the wildflowers or in the songs of the birds. They all seem to be chirping. Even the blooming of an amaryllis in Spring shows forth God's design. Out of one single bud comes four giant blooms. God seemingly makes abundance from little.

Psalms 8:3-6 (KJV)
"When I consider thy heavens, the work of thy fingers, the moon and the stars, which thou hast ordained;

"What is man, that thou art mindful of him? and the son of man, that thou visitest him?

"For thou hast made him a little lower than the angels, and hast crowned him with glory and honor.

"Thou madest him to have dominion over the works of thy hands; thou hast put all things under his feet:"

You have dominion. God created you to be in charge. He has given you authority to take care of whatever challenges face you today. His wisdom is accessible. Go forth with confidence. God made you for this.

Hazel's Gem # 37:
"When the storms of life beat hard
And Satan's darts are hurled
Scripture hidden in the heart
Arise like flags unfurled."

Hazel's Gem # 38:
"God's Word is like a life preserve; it keeps the soul from sinking in the sea of troubles."

When your path seems too crooked; when you don't understand why and all you can do is keep walking even though you can't see the light, the scriptures you have studied will rise up in you and fortify your breaking heart. It is important that you study the Bible. Attending church is vital. Sunday School classes and Bible studies are wonderful places to learn. The more you learn, the better off you are.

If you are walking through a hard place with a loved one, maybe you've walked there for years, the Bible reminds you that you are not alone.

"Yea, though I walk through the valley of the shadow of death, I will fear no evil: for thou art with me; thy rod and thy staff they comfort me.

"Thou preparest a table before me **in the presence** of my enemies: thou anointest my head with oil; my cup runneth over." Psalms 23:4, 5

Jehovah, your creator, is with you in all you face today.

Hazel's Gem # 39:
"By grace one day I came to see
That it would wiser be
To cease my criticizing 'them,'
And right what's wrong with me."

Hazel's Gem # 40: "When you are looking for faults, use a mirror, not a telescope."

It is so very easy to see someone else's short comings, so tempting to point out their inefficiencies. If you will pause and think of your own qualities, you will have less to criticize in someone else. Because you know the reasons behind your actions, and the series of events that happened to you – you always judge yourself less harshly. Examining yourself will help you understand someone else's actions. They don't look so bad, after all.

"And why beholdest thou the mote that is in thy brother's eye, but considerest not the beam that is in thine own eye?

"Or how wilt thou say to thy brother, Let me pull out the mote out of thine eye; and, behold a beam is in thine own eye?

"Thou hypocrite, first cast out the beam out of thine own eye; and then shalt thou see clearly to cast out the mote out of thy brother's eye." Matthew 7: 3, 4, 5

Jesus tells it like it is! Be careful, don't criticize! Today presents a fresh opportunity to be a better you than you were yesterday.

Hazel's Gem # 41:
> "<u>Humility</u> is perpetual quietness of heart. It is to have no trouble, never to be vexed or irritated; to wonder at nothing that is done to me and to feel nothing done against me. It is to be at rest when no one praises me, and when I am blessed or despised to seek a blessed inner closet where I can shut the door and kneel to my Father in secret and be at peace as in a deep sea of calmness when all around is irritation and trouble."

Yikes! That sounds like I am without emotion or feeling, almost like a zombie.

You got it! Paul says in Galatians 2:20a (KJV), "I am crucified with Christ: nevertheless I live; yet not I, but Christ liveth in me…"

Our emotions and feelings become Christ's responses, not ours. It is a miracle. We are able to show restraint, to exhibit love when common sense would say, "They are wrong, they don't deserve it! Defend yourself!" Someone once wrote that a kite flies higher against the wind. Adversity will propel you toward greatness if you allow God's spirit to launch you.

Have a great day, no matter what…Christ liveth in you, if you have accepted Him.

New Horizons for an Old Girl

Alice Hein Schiel

Swimming lets me be without glasses
Swimming makes me feel so light
Tho' mine's the only test I must pass,
Sometimes my chest still feels tight.

At sixty-four I decide to swim
A good decision for me
And I just decided, on a whim,
"Create opportunity."

"Don't sit on the sideline anymore.
A new frontier awaits you!
Jump in the cool water and explore
Buoyancy, drift, backsplash too."

Not all was mastered in six lessons
I did conquer freestyle swim
I practiced, practiced between sessions
Exercising all my limbs.

Swimming on my back is my best tour
At least I gain momentum
For me new skills have opened a door
Friendly water beckons, "Come!"

(Today's challenges are your new victories!)

Hazel's Gem # 42:
"The conversion of a soul is the miracle of a moment, the growth of a saint is the task of a lifetime."

In a moment Jesus changes us from "lost soul" to "child of God!" If we but confess with our mouth the Lord Jesus and believe in our heart that God raised him from the dead, we shall be saved. Romans 10:9 (KJV)

But what is gem #42 talking about? "The growth of a saint," what is that? A saint is defined as 1) a sinless person regarded with deep respect, 2) a person who is unusually charitable and patient, 3) in certain churches a deceased person officially recognized as having lived an exceptionally holy life.

Ephesians 2:19 declares that we are "no more strangers and foreigners, but fellow citizens <u>with the saints</u>, and of the household of God." So, technically, any Christian is called a saint! But to be regarded by others as "saintly" we must show holiness in our daily living. Therein lies the challenge. Don't be discouraged when you don't measure up. Determine that this day you will be more saintly than you were yesterday.

Ephesians 4:12 tells us that God provides apostles, prophets, evangelists, pastors, and teachers to <u>perfect the saints</u> for the work of the ministry. We have to make ourselves available at church meetings for the ministers to train and teach us so we will be perfected.

Yes, we are converted in a moment, but spend the rest of our lives becoming like Jesus.

Hazel's Gem # 43:
"A warm smile and wholesome laughter have great face value."

Live in tune with your creator. Knowing God loves you and cares for you can make you smile when a frown makes more sense. That smile pays off! And it is more than just fewer wrinkles! Let God's inner light shine through. When everything says, "despair," "defeat," "tragedy," "loss;" Jesus in your heart brings a calmness and strength.

Proverbs 15:15b says, "…he that is of a merry heart hath a continual feast." Nehemiah 8:10b declares, "…for the joy of the Lord is your strength."

Rebuilding the walls of Jerusalem began in 445 BC. After Nehemiah and the Israelites finished rebuilding the walls and setting the doors, the people were counted by genealogy in the records. When the seventh month came which was historically their month for the Feasts of Trumpets, the Day of Atonement, and the Feast of Tabernacles, the people asked Ezra the priest to read the book of the Law of Moses to them. At first they stood and lifted their hands to bless God, then they bowed down with faces to the ground and began to weep as the Law was read. Ezra instructed them to "mourn not, nor weep." In verse 10 he continues, "Go your way, eat the fat, drink the sweet drink, … be not grieved, and depressed, for the **joy of the Lord is your strength** and stronghold."

We too must take action to establish and show the joy of the Lord in our lives. Try it today! A merry heart should show up on your face. You will feel God's strength empower you to face your mountains and your devastation and use them to help others.

PS. If you are nervous about a presentation, try flashing a genuine smile. (You may need to practice in front of your mirror if this is new territory for you.) You'll be surprised how your confidence level will go up.

Hazel's Gem # 44:
> "The <u>Bible</u> stands though the hills may tumble
> It will firmly stand when the earth shall crumble
> I will plant my feet on its firm foundation
> For the <u>Bible</u> stands."

You can count on it. The <u>Bible's</u> instructions are always current. They may not be popular, but they provide a firm foundation. The <u>Bible</u> applies to every generation and provides the keys to living in harmony and enjoying peace. It provides the keys to overcoming evil and surviving devastation.

John chapter one tells us that the **Word** was in the beginning, was with God, and was God. Verse 14 declares that the **Word** became flesh and dwelt among us. Jesus is the living word – the word in flesh.

I Peter 1:25 – "But the word of the Lord endureth for ever. And this is the word which by the gospel is preached unto you."

II Timothy 3:16, 17 – "All scripture is given by inspiration of God, and is profitable for doctrine, for reproof, for correction, for instruction in righteousness:

"That the man of God may be perfect, thoroughly furnished unto all good works."

II Peter 1:20, 21 – "Knowing this first, that no prophecy of the scripture is of any private interpretation.

"For the prophecy came not in old time by the will of man: but holy men of God spake as they were moved by the Holy Ghost."

Read it, study it, learn it. Let it become a part of you. You can count on the <u>Bible</u>.

Alice Hein Schiel B.S., M.Ed.

Hazel's Gem # 45:
"Speak, Lord, in the stillness
In the quiet hour
May I feel Thy Presence
Know Thy quickening power."

As you take time to focus on God gather your thoughts. Before you turn on the radio, tv, or your phone listen for His voice in the stillness. Make an effort to wait on Him. There are times when God seems to thunder His presence, but most often He is waiting for us to listen. His message will always be in agreement with the written word, the Bible.

I Kings 19: 11, 12: "And he said, Go forth, and stand upon the mount before the LORD. And, behold, the LORD passed by, and a great and strong wind rent the mountains, and brake in pieces the rocks before the LORD; but the LORD was not in the wind: and after the wind an earthquake; but the LORD was not in the earthquake:

"And after the earthquake a fire; but the LORD was not in the fire: and after the fire a **still small voice.**"

Be alert for that small voice. As you pray sometimes it is appropriate to sing your praise to Him. The Word does say that God dwells in the praises of His people. He will be near you. When we receive Christ, the Spirit comes to dwell in us. As we spend time in prayer, we sense His presence in a greater way.

All this I.C.U. "beeping" for my sister
Dorothy McManners stopped on
May 20, 2018. Dorothy was the first to
encourage me in writing my first book.
Love you, Dee.

I.C.U.

(Intensive Care Unit in Hospital)

In the solitude the beepers sound.
The noise pierces thoughts of peace.
Surely the monitor's squeal is bound
To bring help. Please! Volume cease!

No one answers the monotonous call.
The beep just keeps on singing.
So many bells and whistles! They all
take turns; one's always ringing.

Oxygen level, temperature,
Blood pressure, drainage, heart rate
These signs of life do our hope procure:
nerve-wracking solace; we wait.

The nurse comes in and hustles about.
"It's sort of busy right now.
Someone's going home," she bows, goes out.
Wretched time – you seem so slow!

A covered body is rolling by.
The muffled sound of crying
jolts all my senses to realize
that "going home" meant "dying."

We've heard this symphony for how long?
How long my one's been sleeping?
Oh, piercing bells, keep playing your song.
I'm thankful for this beeping!

Alice Hein Schiel

Hazel's Gem # 46:
"If you can't see the bright side of life,
polish the dull side with thanksgiving and praise."

Keep your smile going. Look for things to be thankful for. When the armadillo keeps rooting up your flowers, be thankful for the ones you planted in pots. Or get a few sturdy pots and plant some flowers in them. When your paycheck doesn't reach to cover all the needs, be thankful for the bills you did pay. Go over your budget again and ask God to help you find expenses to trim. (One big thing is eating out. Taking a sandwich or leftovers for lunch can help your food bill. Try planning a weekly dinner menu to keep you from rushing for the convenience of fast food.)

When you can't get your hair to look good, be thankful that you have some hair! When your walls need paint but there is no money for paint, rejoice that you have walls!

Make an effort to be enthusiastic. H.W. Arnold said, "The worst bankruptcy in the world is the person who has lost their enthusiasm. Let someone lose everything else in the world but their enthusiasm and they will come through again to success."

"Never lag in **zeal** and in earnest endeavor; be **aglow** and burning with the Spirit, serving the Lord." Romans 12:11 (Amplified Bible)

Hazel's Gem # 47:
> "One candle set against the dark
> Can be a beacon in the night
> To draw me homeward by its light
> Though it is but a tiny spark."

People are always watching you. Some are looking for opportunity to put you down. Others are sincerely looking for a good example in this world where evil seems to be flaunted and people who walk "after the flesh" are lifted up.

You are influencing those you come in contact with. The people in your neighborhood, your children, your co-workers, and friends need a steady example. One of the hardest times to remain a good example is when you are being corrected. Correction may be from your boss, your pastor, or a friend. How do you react?

When things are darkest around you is when your candle shines brightest. Two scriptures really highlight this topic.

"He who refuses and ignores instruction and correction despises himself, but he who heeds reproof gets understanding." Proverbs 15:32 (Amp)

"Those whom I [dearly and tenderly] love, I tell their faults and convict and convince and reprove and chasten [I discipline and instruct them]. So be enthusiastic and in earnest and burning with zeal and repent [changing your mind and attitude]." Revelation 3:19 (Amplified Bible)

Be pliable in God's hands. You can trust Him. Your reactions will help others see how they should respond when facing correction themselves. Light the way.

Alice Hein Schiel B.S., M.Ed.

Hazel's Gem # 48:
"Money doesn't buy happiness;
It only pays for the illusion."

Priorities! Priorities! Having things doesn't mean you are happy. A healthy life is more than a big bank account or many bank accounts! A healthy life means you take care of your relationship with God; you seek Him. A healthy life means that your family feels loved and is not pushed aside. A healthy life means that you take care of your body – you eat good foods and you exercise. A healthy life means you earn enough money so that all your needs are met, you can give to others, and you can save for the future. It is nice to have a lot of things, but do not make things your focus.

I heard our society described like this:

"When we are young we sacrifice our health to earn money. When we are old we spend all our money trying to buy our health."

Don't let that be your story.

"But lay not up for yourselves treasure upon earth, where moth and rust doth corrupt, and where thieves break through and steal:

"But lay up for yourselves treasures in heaven, where neither moth nor rust doth corrupt, and where thieves do not break through nor steal:" Matt. 6: 19, 20 (KJV)

Wishing you a truly happy, healthy life, not just a bunch of stuff!

Hazel's Gem # 49:
"It is hard to tune in on Heaven's message
If our lives are full of earthly static."

Our five senses (sight, hearing, smelling, tasting, touching) allow us to enjoy and respond to the world around us. Sometimes these receptors put us on overload. It's hard to process everything that we receive and doubts creep in. We must deal with our doubts.

I recently heard Dr. Tom Sigley, Pastor of CROSSROADS Christian Fellowship in Union, New Jersey address this issue. He said that the remedy to doubt is FAITH. "Faith is not subjective feelings; faith is not a blind leap into the dark; faith is not positive thinking; faith is not presumption. Faith is choosing to believe that the scriptures are true; faith is confidence in God; faith is knowing that God is for us and will deliver."

How do we get rid of some of the static in our lives? We control what our senses are exposed to: choose friends wisely, read and listen to positive, appropriate sources. Don't click on every article that flashes by when you are online! Control your time.

Every man has faith and will believe in something. "…God has dealt to every man the measure of faith." Romans 12:3c (KJV) Take time to read the Bible. Nurture your faith in God.

Alice Hein Schiel B.S., M.Ed.

"The flowers lost the battle"

Vandal in the Night

Alice Hein Schiel

I delight in beautiful flowers.
It seems that they speak to me.
I always succumb to the power
of a bloom that smiles with glee.

I faithfully work to till the soil,
control the weeds, and water.
Flowers responding to all my toil,
stretched t'ward the sun cry, "Hotter!"

Nightfall slips in and I take a rest.
My pillow's so inviting.
But someone's out there making a mess.
My dreams conceal the fighting.

The morning light reveals the sad tale.
The flowers lost the battle.
Uprooted, they are so thin and frail!
Can't be solved with a paddle!

The culprit? He is not to be seen.
He sleeps for twenty-three hours,
then roams and roots wherever he deems
looking for grubs, insects, sours.

His tricky nose is a pointed cone
which assaults my small plants. Oh!!
"Guess we'll have to build a fence," I moan,
"That pesky armadillo!"

Hazel's Gem # 50:
"The desire to make restitution is one of the sure signs of regeneration."

As you follow Jesus you will become more like him.

A friend of mine worked for a large company. If my friend needed a tool at home, he would take one to use. Of course, he conveniently "forgot" to return the tools he took. My friend said that, eventually, for most of the tools the company had, he had one at home. After dedicating his life to Jesus, he began to feel guilty about the tools he had stolen. No person said anything to him, but the Holy Spirit inside him kept whispering, "You need to take those tools back." One day he packed up all the tools and returned them to the tool room. The man who was in charge gasped! He was astonished! The other workers may not have known what had happened, but my friend received peace, knowing he had obeyed the voice of God.

In Luke chapter 19, a short tax collector climbed a tree to see Jesus. Jesus noticed him in the tree and instructed him to come down. Zaccheus was forever changed! In verse 8, Zaccheus declared, "…if I have taken any thing from any man by false accusation, I restore him fourfold." Regeneration led Zaccheus to restitution. He paid back what he took wrongfully.

Hazel's Gem # 51:
> "Look not on outward form,
> its beauty may depart.
> But look instead for faith and truth
> that lie within the heart."

That's very good advice for the one looking for a mate for life! Make your choice based on the inner person. Look past the beautiful eyes and seek a heart that is following after God. Watch for kindness, patience, and self-control. Outward beauty changes. Ten years from now an ordinary face may have grown beautiful or handsome. A beautiful face may have become worn or scarred. Fall in love with the person under that skin.

Gem # 51 is also very comforting advice for those growing old. It's comforting to know that in spite of your collection of age spots, your inner self can grow to be more like Jesus. A joyful heart shows up in a smile that adds a glow to even the most wrinkled face. It can be seriously depressing when your "heretofore toned" body begins to sag. Mirrors seem to become the enemy. It is so seriously refreshing to remember that "I will be changed…in the twinkling of an eye." I Corinthians 15:52 declares it. The real you lives inside that body. Your true beauty is in your heart. Enjoy that news today! Your future is bright!

Hazel's Gem # 52:
"Discontent makes rich men poor,
while contentment makes poor men rich."

Always wanting to be on top or first can lead to despair. Many work to earn position or fame. They keep working for one thing and then another and never stop to enjoy the moment, the things already accomplished. They feel unfulfilled and insecure when the truth is they are richer than most people in the world. Don't be caught in this trap. Success is being able to sing whatever your circumstance may be.

The Apostle Paul had much to say about contentment, "I have learned, in whatsoever state I am, therewith to be content." Philippians 4: 11. Paul relied on Jesus to give him strength in every situation. He went on to say, "I know both how to be abased and I know how to abound." He was thankful in every moment. Right now, think of something to be thankful for (a new day, fresh air, a car to drive, clean water in your home). Having a family is a blessing, but if you don't have one, Christian friends can be your joy. Paul faced imprisonment, loneliness, and hunger with the same commitment to his calling that he exhibited when he was treated as a god, admired by many, and provided with plenty. Things were never his motivation. His inner strength came from Christ.

Contentment contributes to good health. Get home from work as quickly as you can. Sacrificing your health by constantly working long hours will result in poor health. Take care of yourself. Plan time to relax. Attending church is a great way to pause and let your mind find peace.

Hazel's Gem # 53:
"To enjoy our standing in Christ, we must learn the secret of walking with Christ."

The scripture tells us that there are blessings found in walking with God. Psalms 91 says that "he who dwells in the secret place of the most high shall abide under the shadow of the Almighty." The chapter goes on to list numerous blessings, many of which paint a picture of God as our great protector. He shields us from all that life throws at us. He is our refuge, our fortress; we do not have to be afraid.

Because our walk with God is a spiritual journey we don't always understand. This is a journey of faith: many never find the path even though it is the most important journey of our lives. It is our nature to try to find something that makes more sense, something that will answer all our questions.

Werner Heisenberg, the father of Quantum Physics, said this, "The first gulp of the glass of natural sciences will make you an atheist, but at the bottom of the glass God is waiting for you."

Walk with Christ today. John 4:24(KJV) "God is a Spirit: and they that worship him must worship him in spirit and in truth."

Slandered, but I'm okay!

Slandered

I sit here in the quiet, thinking.
What a beautiful day it was!
But words jumped out like lights a-blinking,
carving my heart as a knife does.

It seems they are all against me now.
Things did get reversed so quickly:
nasty words, an arrogance pow-wow.
Hurt, confused, I feel so sickly.

Rejection rises; I fight the tears.
Tortured as they speak against me.
It seems I'm drowning, hurt so severe.
What do they think? Can they not see?

Floundering 'tween my faith and hatred
my soul cries out to God above,
"Lord, separate what's junk, what's sacred!
Deliver me by your great love."

"Wash my wounds, healing them so gently;
Remembering I'm made from dust.
Please set my feet; hold me steadfastly!
I choose to smile; I will adjust."

Up ahead are those who love me.
I'm tougher now than yesterday.
Though slandered by words, maliciously.
My heart's been freed and I'm okay.

Alice Hein Schiel

Hazel's Gem # 54:
"If you are wearing a spirit of heaviness,
try a garment of praise."

Sometimes it's hard to focus as you begin your day. Thoughts race, imaginations barge in, you say things that reveal your inner fears, your spirit sags.

No, you are not hopeless; you are not defeated! You are a usually confident human facing situations you've never encountered before. Step back and make a conscious decision to cast off the fear as if it were a garment. Take control. Remember that you are never immune to tricks of the devil. But he is defeated and you can conquer anything if you let God be your guide.

Isaiah 61:3 declares that you should put on "the garment of praise for the spirit of heaviness." You can receive "beauty for ashes" and "the oil of joy for mourning." What a great exchange! Begin to sing praises to God. Lift up your voice. Sing any praise song you know. If you can't think of one, just make one up. "God is so good. He is my father. He is the almighty creator!" Keep it going and you will soon feel the heaviness lift from you. The scripture tells us that God dwells in the praises of His people.

Pastor Ken Teese reminds us, "Man can't stop God's work in your life nor His work on your behalf." Rejoice in this fact! Let the self-condemnation go. You are a child of the king!

Hazel's Gem # 55:
> " 'No condemnation.' Precious word
> Consider it, my soul.
> Thy sins were all on Jesus laid
> His stripes have made thee whole."

"No condemnation!" What a wonderful thought! The Father God looks at you through Jesus' blood which has supernatural power to wipe away all your sin. You are cleansed, freed from all guilt. Take action. Place your faith in Jesus and don't look back. Your friends may remember the wrong you've done; your family may bring it up; society may make you pay; but God wipes your slate clean! You can begin again. The scripture says that your sins are placed in the sea of God's forgetfulness. Forgiveness of sin is the greatest of all miracles. Accept it.

Open your mouth and declare it. "If thou shalt confess with thy mouth the Lord Jesus and shalt believe in thy heart that God hath raised him from the dead, thou shalt be saved." Romans 10:9 (KJV)

But suppose that you've walked with Jesus awhile and now you've sinned; your heart feels dirty. There is a plan! I John 1:9 "If we <u>confess</u> our sins, he is faithful and just and will <u>forgive</u> us our sins and <u>purify</u> us from all unrighteousness." Wow! Have an "uncondemned" day, you spotless child of God.

Hazel's Gem # 56:
"Do what you can, where you are, with what you have."

No dreaming of pie in the sky: if I had this, I'd do this. Take the crumb that is in your hand and use it. You can always give a kind word or a bit of time.

A young man worked at his job to provide for his wife and two small children. He gave his tithe (one tenth of his earnings, see Malachi chapter 10) to the church and paid the bills. He faithfully saved of the little left over and at the end of the year was able to bless his family with a small vacation. He wanted a happy wife, but seldom had cash for flowers or candy so he wrote short love notes and drew a few hearts. The wife was diligent to prepare meals at home. By not "eating out" the couple was able to give to the missionary fund at church.

The mother wanted to be sure that the kids' Sunday School classes were tops so she volunteered as a class assistant. She wanted her home to be well kept, but had no money for maid service so she cleaned weekly. The kids' play brought clutter daily. She decided to teach the kids a clean-up song and they learned to pick up their toys each evening.

They both wanted to live in a Christian nation so they registered to vote, and faithfully voted. He later ran for office.

"Whatever your hand finds to do, do it with all your might..."

Ecclesiastes 9:10 a (Amplified Bible)

Hazel's Gem # 57:
"Walk in His way, thy path shall be
Peaceful, serene, and bright
For God by grace shall dwell in thee
And make thy life a light."

You are a light! Along your journey remember to stay on God's pathway. You will find peace and walk serenely no matter the storms around you. The path will be bright. He will guide you through the hard decisions. Acknowledge Him and He will help you make the right decisions. The path will be illuminated.

God's presence is in you and others see you as a light helping them through dark places.

"Ye are the light of the world. A city that is set on an hill cannot be hid.

"Neither do men light a candle, and put it under a bushel, but on a candlestick; and it giveth light unto all that are in the house.

"Let your light so shine before men, that they may see your good works and glorify your Father which is in heaven." Matthew 5:14-16

You are a light! The things you do today will cause someone to see God. Your reactions and attitudes will help others know how to respond when they face similar challenges. Jesus is shining through you.

Little Chick-a-dee

You thought you really clipped my wings;
You thought my dreams had died;
And when my eyes cried big ol' tears
You were very satisfied.

You didn't know the strength inside
this little chickadee.
A breaking heart, a challenged will
Brought out God's strength in me.

You thought you threw me to the wind,
But 'twas a launch for me!
In case you hear a fl-ut-ter
Look up! It might be me!

'Cause I'm soarin' up against the sky!
I've got me a real good view of
how and what and why.
I'm soarin' – in spite of gravity!
Who'd of ever thought it so – this
Little ol' chick-a dee!

As a hunter wounds a bird in flight,
That's how you wounded me.
You thought that I would spend my time
in fear and self-pity.

But I have got my head up high.
My wings are workin' too-
I very seldom have the time
To even think of you.

You thought you threw me to the wind
But you just set me free.
In case you hear a fl-ut-ter,
Look up – it might be me!

'Cause I'm soarin' up against the sky!
I've got me a real good view of
how and what and why.
I'm soarin' – in spite of gravity!
Who'd of ever thought it so – this
Little ol' chick-a-dee!

(I've read that a chickadee is a small bird that doesn't actually fly, but flutters from tree to tree. The miracle here is that this chickadee is flying like an eagle! I wrote this at a time when I had experienced rejection and hurt. It was actually a song. I would sing it to remind myself that I was free from any and all discouragement that satan or human actions would try to bring against me.) You are free too!

Alice Hein Schiel

Hazel's Gem # 58:
"We are never too old to be happy and glad
To laugh and to smile and to sing.
Never too old for childlike trust
That a blessing each day will bring."

This is a wonderful day to reflect on God's goodness to you. Make a mental list of God's blessings. If possible, speak them out loud. If your current circumstances are bad, go back to the time He healed you, the time He answered your prayer, the time you felt His presence as you walked through tragedy.

"You are as happy as you want to be." Have you ever heard that one? Remember your salvation! That will stir up your joy. Adults are not as care free as children unless they learn to include God every day and trust Him as a child trusts. Ask God to anoint you for this day's challenges. He will!

In II Chronicles Hanani reminded righteous King Asa that God was wanting to help him, but he had looked to the king of Syria. Chapter 16, verse 9a says, "For the eyes of the Lord run to and fro throughout the whole earth to show Himself strong in behalf of those whose hearts are blameless toward Him." (Amplified Bible) Your heart is blameless because of Jesus. It's time to laugh, to smile, to sing! Trust God!

Hazel's Gem # 59:
"A true friend will put a finger on your faults without rubbing them in."

You know those people! You love them! They value you for no reason. They have no hidden agendas, just honest friendship. They bring a smile to your face. They always nudge you in the right direction but never take advantage of you when you're down, when you're wrong, or when you have failed.

This kind of friend has been forgiven and has learned to forgive. Pastor John Mark Caton has a sermon called "God, Love, and Duct tape" which points listeners to these three dynamics:

1) Don't live a jealous or envious life!
2) Don't live your life angry with others!
3) Don't forget to forgive a lot! (Be "duct tape" for others.)

"Love bears up under anything and everything that comes, is ever ready to believe the best of every person, its hopes are fadeless under all circumstances, and it endures everything [without weakening]." I Cor. 13:7 (Amp.)

"Confess to one another therefore your faults (your slips, your false steps, your offenses, your sins) and pray [also] for one another, that you may be healed and restored [to a spiritual tone of mind and heart]." James 5:16a (Amp.)

You love a friend who sees the best in you. Watch for an opportunity to be this type of friend today.

Hazel's Gem # 60:
"The Gospel can break hard hearts and heal broken ones."

The message of Jesus has the power to mend every person. It becomes a hammer or a balm. This is a supernatural thing accomplished by the Holy Spirit who blows upon the inner part of man. The Spirit brings the power of Jesus which can resurrect the human spirit and renew the soul, the heart of man.

In Luke chapter 20 Jesus told the parable of the wicked husbandmen. The chief priests and scribes perceived that he had spoken the parable against them. He ended the story with words about himself. "…The stone which the builders rejected, the same is become the head of the corner? Whosoever shall fall upon that stone shall be broken, but on whomsoever it shall fall, it will grind him to powder." Luke 20: 17b,18 (KJV) If your heart is hard it's better to offer yourself to him. Ezekiel 36:26 says God can take away the stony heart and give you a "heart of flesh."

In Luke 4:18a Jesus declares, "The Spirit of the Lord is upon me, because he hath anointed me to preach the gospel to the poor; he hath sent me to heal the brokenhearted…" Healing broken hearts was His mission on Earth, the very reason He came. If you are bruised or crushed He has the power to make you whole.

Jesus is the answer for every heart.

Hazel's Gem # 61:
"The test of your Christianity is
what you do in your spare time."

Frequently I see folks grab their cellphones when downtime appears. Some like to outdo their current record on games. Others seize the opportunity to check Facebook. It's great to be connected, but our most important connection is not with humans, it's our supernatural lifeline – with God. Alright! I know we can't always be talking to God, or can we? Paul wrote that we should "pray without ceasing." I Thessalonians 5:17. Of course, he also included in this chapter that we should "rejoice evermore," and "give thanks in everything." I understand this as meaning that our communication with God is always open. We can <u>talk</u> to Him at any second and whatever we are <u>doing</u> reflects that.

We should live a life of stewardship. If you enjoy watching TV or going to the movie for relaxation make sure that you are feeding yourself with shows that build up your spirit. When gaming, select games that are not promoting evil. If you work in the yard or the garden make sure you plant only plants listed in the <u>Bible</u>. NOT! We don't have to be "nutso," but "everyone of us shall give account of himself to God." Romans 14:12. Judge yourself.

Spare time? You could choose to speak to a coworker, smile at your spouse, hold the door for an older person, or visit a widow.

Alice Hein Schiel B.S., M.Ed.

Christmas Thoughts

by Sarah Muñoz, Dec. 2006

With the birth of my little grandson, Aiden, I have marveled again at the miracle of birth and God's design. Seeing him at Christmastime has brought these thoughts to mind about the One whose birthday we celebrate:

Tiny helpless baby.
That's what God became so that we could become overcomers, more than conquerors, always victorious, triumphant! O the depth of the wisdom of God, the majesty of the mystery! Who would have thought that God would become incarnate? Who would have thought that still today He desires to live in houses of clay?

Tiny baby face.
Little eyes learning to see. Amazing that the God who could see all the way from eternity past through the present into eternity future would limit himself to a few inches of vision, searching His mother's face. He did it so we could see past the temporal into the eternal and so that our vision would be focused on His face.

Little tiny hands.
The one whose hands measured the heavens with a span and the waters of the ocean in His palm now with hands so tiny that they could grasp His mother's finger and be filled. Marveled over that they could be so tiny, yet so perfect. He did it so that we could marvel that our hands could be made holy hands, that we could lay hold on eternal life, that we could grasp eternity.

Christmas Thoughts
by Sarah Muñoz (cont'd)

Little feet.
Perfectly formed, made according to His own design. He walked in the dust and dirt and mud so that we could walk in purity and holiness. Left unwashed by Simon, washed with the tears of the harlot, dried by her hair, kissed in worship. Pierced by the nails, fastened to the cross. He walked on earth so that we could walk in heaven.

Tiny baby, lying in a manger.
God omnipotent, veiled in flesh. He became weak so that we could be strong—filled with power. Very life itself came to die that we might live.

Tiny baby.
Great Redeemer. Wonderful Savior.
Coming King.
My Jesus.

(My sister Sarah's grandson was born prematurely, weighing 1 pound and 15 ounces! He was 12 inches long. He was due in October, but was born in July. I love these words that stirred within her as she contemplated this miracle. Aiden is at this writing a whole and healthy young man! Read this prose once more with these things on your mind and let it sink in: God, a baby. I hope you enjoy this piece as much as I do!)

Alice Hein Schiel B.S., M.Ed.

Hazel's Gem # 62:
"Attending services doesn't depend on how far one lives from the church, but how close he lives to God."

When you choose to follow God you are in covenant with him. You bring to him your brokenness, your human talents, your best, your obedience in exchange for his forgiveness, his prosperity, his life, his blessing on your family and your possessions. Deuteronomy 28:6 says that the Israelites would be blessed when they came in and when they went out. Verse 7 declares that their enemies would flee before them. Verse 13 says that the Lord would make them "the head and not the tail"; they would be "above only, and not beneath" if they observed and obeyed the commandments of their God. In the New Covenant we enjoy these blessings through Jesus.

One of the signs to everyone around that the Israelites were in covenant with Jehovah God was the Sabbath. "Moreover also I gave them my Sabbaths to be a sign between me and them, that they might know that I am the Lord that sanctify them." Ezekiel 20:12 (KJV) Christians no longer observe the Sabbath (Saturday), but Sunday is the day set aside to gather with other believers in worship. It is still a sign to God that we are keeping our part of the covenant.

If you have to work on Sunday, choose another time to keep his "Sabbath" each week.

Hazel's Gem # 63:
> "In looking back across my life and all I've lost or made
> I can't recall a single time when fury ever paid;
> I have learned by sad experience that when my temper flies
> I never do a worthy thing, a decent thing, or wise."

It's time to calm down. Reassess your feelings. Quiet your temper. Don't be caught off guard. You know situations will arise; be prepared to deal with stuff. Your emotions don't have to be dead, just controlled.

"He that hath no rule over his own spirit is like a city that is broken down, and without walls." Proverbs 25:28 (KJV)

A city whose walls were broken down was easy prey to the enemy. Armies could walk right in. Thieves had easy access to plunder the goods of the citizens. When your temper flies, your mind becomes easy prey for ungodly thoughts. When you open your mouth in anger you become a target. Your peace is gone. It's impossible to gather up all those words and take back those regretted actions. Learn to rule your temper. It is an art that you will be so glad you acquired!

"He that is slow to anger is better than the mighty; and he that ruleth his spirit than he that taketh a city." Proverbs 16:32

Alice Hein Schiel B.S., M.Ed.

Hazel's Gem # 64:
"Salvation is free, but discipleship is costly!"

Salvation is free to all who believe in Jesus. Jesus' followers became his disciples. They believed his teachings, rested in his sacrifice, absorbed his spirit, and imitated his example. A disciple gives up his goals and takes on the goals of the master. A disciple gives up his rights in order to demonstrate love, joy, peace, patience, gentleness, goodness, meekness, temperance, and faith of the master – not an easy thing! Some, like Mother Theresa, walk away from wealth to embrace poverty. Some have had to walk away from friends (who were actually detrimental).

All of man's glory – his best – is like a flower of grass that drops off as the grass fades away. I Peter 1:24 tells us this. But the Word of the Lord endures forever. The true riches are unseen; they are within you. The seed of eternal life is planted in you when you receive Jesus. It is a priceless treasure. What was sacrificial results in blessing.

Phillip Baker teaches a seminar entitled "The Father's love is unconditional, His blessings are very much conditional." "Love the Lord with all your heart, soul, and mind and love your neighbor as yourself," were Jesus' highest standards. These are recorded in several places including Matthew 22: 37 – 39 (KJV). Look for ways to be this love today.

Hazel's Gem # 65:
> " 'No gain!' I said, but I forgot my Father's faithful word that all things work for blessings here to them that love the Lord."

I feel so downright rotten today. I hope you don't, but I do. Sort of a pity party, I guess. I feel rejected, cast aside like an ole worn out something. But, hey, at least my troubles are not broadcast on the TV screen for all the world to analyze!! (pause) I've had enough of this crying. It's back to me, myself, and I. No one can change how I feel, but me. No one can change how I act, but me. No one cares anyway. The world keeps turning so I'd better hop on or it will roll without me.

"I can do all things through Christ which strengthens me." Phil. 4:13 (KJV) The Amplified <u>Bible</u> says that Christ infuses inner strength into me: <u>"I am self-sufficient in Christ's sufficiency."</u> Wow! I need some of that!

King David lamented, but encouraged himself. "For <u>I will delight myself</u> in your commandments which I love." Psalms 119:47 (Amp.) There is a time to encourage and edify one another (I Thess. 5:11), but now it's time to <u>encourage myself</u>.

"May the God of peace Himself sanctify you ... and may your spirit, and soul, and body be preserved sound and complete [and found] <u>blameless</u>..."

I Thess. 5:23 Amp

I take it!

Claim it for yourself too! We are sanctified and preserved blameless. Rejoice! What a great day this is!

Amazing!

I was studying the reign of Jehoshaphat.
What does it take to have a vict'ry like that,
Where God Himself destroys your enemy
A massive conquest for all to see?

Hezekiah the King did seek God too.
He led all of Judah to worship God anew.
They brought massive offerings including some beasts,
Cleansed the temple, honored God with a feast.

God sent His angel to fight for these kings.
They received not just help, but supernatural things.
They looked in the scripture to find God's word.
Then did what it said, with one accord.

These kings turned their hearts and the hearts of their people
To obey God and honor His steeple.
They put aside their sinful pleasure
To dedicate their lives by ev'ry measure.

God rewarded their pure devotion.
Obedience paid – He calmed the commotion.
Let's try it!! Trust Him! Give Him our attention!
Expecting to reap divine intervention!

Alice Hein Schiel

"For <u>I will delight myself</u> in your commandments, which I love." Psalms 119:47.

Hazel's Gem # 66:
>"We mutter and sputter, we fume and we spurt;
>We mumble and grumble, our feelings get hurt;
>We can't understand things, our vision grows dim
>When all that we need is communion with Him."

Don't let those dark clouds hang around. Refuse to be paralyzed or blinded by situations or circumstances. Get into the Word and read where Paul focused on God.

"…we consider and look not to the things that are seen but to the things that are unseen; for the things that are visible are temporal (brief and fleeting), but the things that are invisible are deathless and everlasting." II Corinthians 4:18 (Amp.)

The prophet Jeremiah, whose heart was broken to see the ruins of Jerusalem, encourages us, "It is because of the Lord's mercy and loving-kindness that we are not consumed, because His [tender] compassions fail not. They are new every morning;" Lamentations 3:22, 23a. (Amp.) Be aware of His presence.

Mike Murdock says that we should "make a decision to look for divine rewards in every battle." You are stepping into something new and the enemy is feeling left out so he tries to deter you. Press on to victory! Pray, recognizing God as your source, declaring His triumph over all confusion. Let His peace flood you as you take time to focus on Him. Walk, dance in the light of His faithfulness.

Hazel's Gem # 67:
"Speak up for Christ: silence isn't always Golden;
Sometimes it may be just plain yellow!"

Speaking up for Christ doesn't always mean preaching a sermon. You can speak up for moral excellence by not laughing when dirty jokes are shared.

There was a major test scheduled for Physics class. Someone stole the test and secretly presented copies to the class. Just saying, "No, thanks," when the stolen test was offered for study was a way of speaking up for Christ. Jesus said we are "the salt of the earth." Matt. 5:13. We preserve the earth. Refusing to be part of sinful activities shouts truth loudly.

I remember a time when I was very nervous about speaking out. My pastor was preparing to preach the funeral of a close acquaintance who had committed suicide. During my morning devotion time a scripture seemed to leap at me. I felt that it was for the pastor. There were many thoughts screaming at me to remain silent: 1) He is my spiritual leader, why would I advise him? 2) I will be saying that God has spoken to little ole' me. 3) What if he doesn't receive it?

I decided to listen to the still small voice within and not be a chicken! My pastor did receive the scripture. It became one of his texts for the funeral.

Speak up for Christ. Don't be yellow!

Hazel's Gem # 68:
"You cannot 'starve' a man who is feeding on God's word."

When you walk with God and regularly read his book you enter into a supernatural realm. No matter what you're facing there's a promise to cover it!

If you're starving **socially** – no friends, people against you, Proverbs 18:24b "There is a friend who sticks closer than a brother." God is such a friend.

If you're starving **emotionally** – you feel abandoned; you've cried until there are no more tears, Psalms 27:10, "When my father and my mother forsake me, then the Lord will take me up."

If you are starving **physically** – no food to eat, Psalms 103:5 The Lord "satisfieth thy mouth with good things; so that thy youth is renewed like the eagle's." Psalms 119:103 thy words are "sweeter than honey to my mouth!"

If you're starving **spiritually** – you're disconnected from believers which is where life flows, Jesus said in John 4:32, "I have meat to eat that ye know not of."

If you're starving **financially** – not enough money for your bills, Malachi 3:10-12 tells you to bring your tithes (1/10 of your income) to God's house and prove God in His promise to pour out a great blessing on you and to rebuke the devourer for your sake.

The Word is life. You can have as much of it as you are willing to take in. No one can starve you when you are "eating" regularly!

Alice Hein Schiel B.S., M.Ed.

Love...is kind

Hazel's Gem # 69:
"Do a deed of simple kindness
Though its end you may not see…"

I have received many acts of kindness, and two of these are etched in my memory. It happened the summer that I turned 13. Services and activities at church camp were divided into two groups: kids aged 9 to 12 and those aged 13 to 19. At 13 I had made it into the "teenage" realm, but was on the bottom rung.

When we arrived at camp it was raining. I took my shoes off because I didn't want to get them all muddy and wet. I put them in the shoebox and ran to check-in. Later, to my dismay, I discovered that I'd left my shoebox inside my parents' car!! In it were my only pair of **shoes** and **my spending money**! My heart sank. I was facing a whole week with no shoes and no snacks. Oh well, I was excited to be at camp. On Monday morning Hazel Flora, my counselor, said to me, "I will pay you ten cents if you will make my bed." Hazel paid me ten cents each day to make her bed. Kindness! Hello, snack shack!

Going all week with no shoes was embarrassing. My friend Gayle Yarborough who was from Humble, Texas decided that she would go barefoot with me everywhere, all week! Major Kindness! Thank you, Gayle! I have never forgotten your kindness.

"Love … is kind" I Cor. 13:4. Be uncommonly kind. Make someone's day!

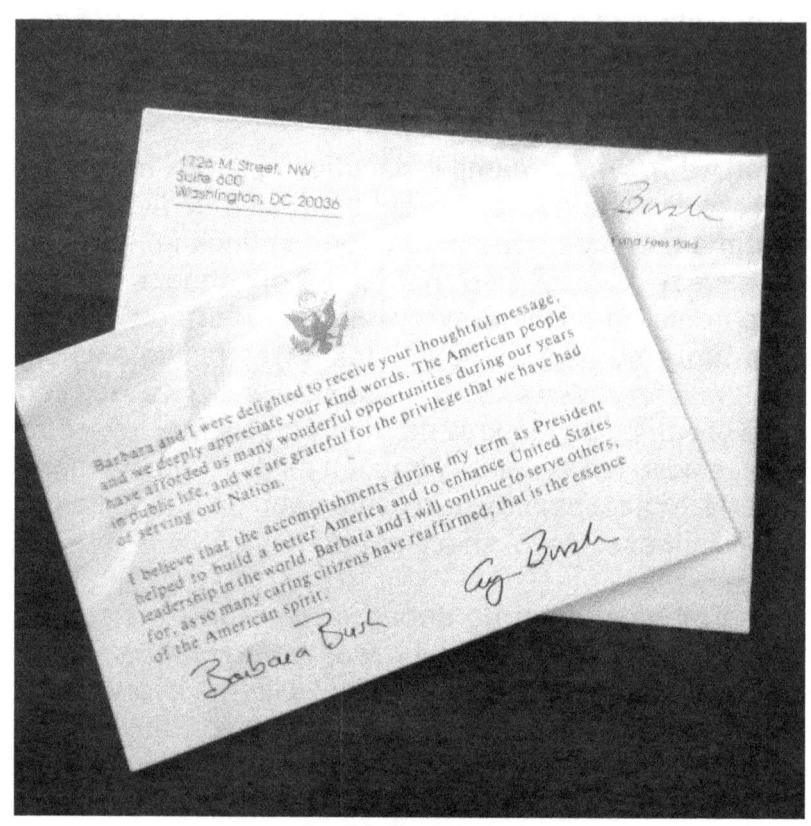

I'm one of millions, but just the same!

Barbara Bush

Alice Hein Schiel

I didn't know her, but I thought I did
Famous woman, white hair on her head.
She wore solid colors, pearls of white.
Stomped on illiteracy, the blight!

Prim and proper – didn't care about looks.
Her life's mission was all about books.
Mother of six; loved more than her own.
Wanted all to read; goals etched in stone.

I didn't know her, but it seemed I did.
Her short laugh, that familiar white head.
Once First Lady, thus celebrity!
Name in news, now occasionally.

Always supporting the Houston teams;
Her smiling face on stadium screens.
Once sent me a card; it's in a frame.
I'm one of millions, but just the same….

I didn't know her; but maybe I do…
Allegiance to country – red, white, and blue.
Firm faith in God, commitment that's true,
Strong love for fam'ly, friends old and new.

She'd no fear of death, a calm peace of mind.
Wit, humor; home in Heaven to find.

Hazel's Gem # 70:
"Think less of the power of things over you and more of the power of Christ in you."

Things possess us only to the degree we allow. Jesus Christ provided power to us through His conquering death. I John 4:4: "Ye are of God, little children, and have overcome them: because greater is he that is in you, than he that is in the world."

Such a powerful truth this is! Remind yourself of it as often as you need to. Christ in you is greater than any challenge you face. Say it aloud, "Greater is he (Christ) that is in me than he (Satan) that is in the world." Pray it during your devotional time.

The responsibilities of life can weigh you down. Those appliances you need and love bring frustration when they break. Additional chores (doing dishes by hand, taking clothes to the washateria, etc.) steal your time. When you realize Christ's power within to help you deal with mess, doing dishes by hand becomes time to sing! The washateria becomes your ministry opportunity for the day, or the week, or the month! Spread sunshine as you go there. Let Christ in you shine through. Waiting for your vehicle to be fixed allows interaction with someone new. You have power in you to overcome any frustration!

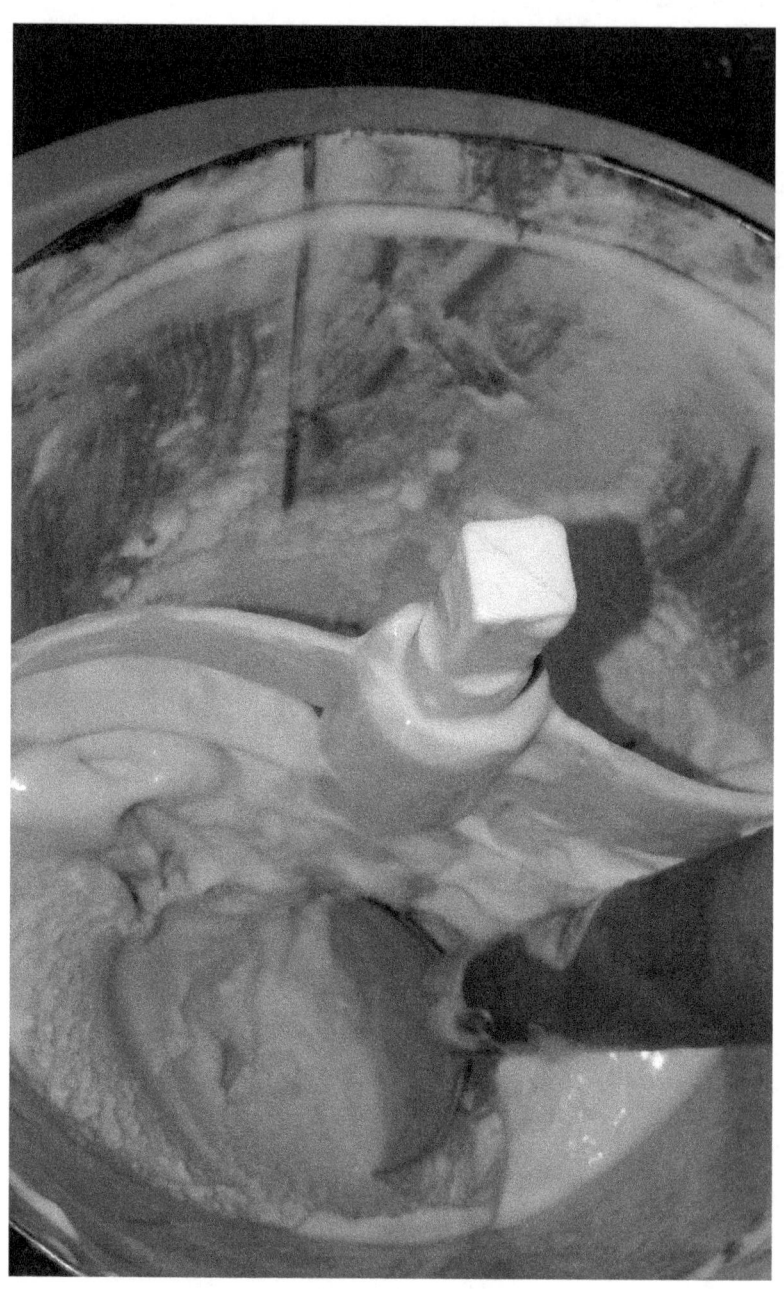

Homemade Ice Cream

Hazel's Gem # 71:
"The man who only samples God's Word occasionally will never acquire much of a taste for it."

"It's hard to read and too confusing," the timid and the weak declare about the <u>Bible</u>. Such words hold little credibility today. The <u>Bible</u> is available in various translations which bypass the "Elizabethan English" of the King James Bible. The Living Bible, The Message, The New International Version (NIV), and the Amplified Bible are just a few of the easier to understand versions.

God's Word tells of his kingdom which is like a treasure hidden in a field (Matthew 13:44). When it's discovered, a man will sell everything to purchase it. You have to <u>keep digging</u> to get to a treasure. You will discover that God's testimonies are "sweeter also than honey and the honeycomb." Psalm 19:10b. Keep reading to find the hidden treasure.

It's better than discovering ice cream! I think of Hazel's ice cream recipe – so simple, yet so sweet – you want more of it!

Hazel's Ice Cream
3 c. sugar
6 eggs
2 TB vanilla
1 can condensed milk (Eagle Brand)

Mix thoroughly and pour into your ice cream freezer, finish filling with whole milk; then freeze according to directions.

(If you're dieting or can't eat sugar, ignore the recipe! Read more! God's word is sugar free and no calories!)

Hazel's Gem # 72:
"He who puts God first will be truly happy at the Last."

Today's writing will really get you excited! Discovering God's will for the "whole man" puts you in a powerful place. God has redeemed your spirit by Jesus' atoning death. But he has also provided a way for health and prosperity. It's up to <u>you</u>!

"Some trust in chariots and some in horses; but we will remember the name of the Lord our God." Psalm 20:7. David knew that even in battle victory does not come only because of superior military equipment; it comes because of trust in God.

Whatever battles you face today, call on the name of the Lord your God. Jehovah will give you the victory. He can help you get your reports done, pass that inspection, balance that spreadsheet, or make that presentation. In verse 8 (Amplified) David declares that those who trusted in their might "are bowed down and fallen; but <u>we are risen</u> and stand upright."

You can walk in victory each and every day. The key is to feed your soul (your mind, emotions, and will) with God's values.

III John 2 states, "Beloved, I pray that you may prosper in <u>all</u> things and be in health, just as your soul prospers." Is God speaking to you about feeding your soul? Listen! Remember, God doesn't bring condemnation, but He does bring conviction to move you in the right direction.

Hazel's Gem # 73:
"The Bible has survived the ignorance of its friends and the hatred of its enemies."

The Bible is a great treasure in the fact that God inspired men to write it.

(II Peter 1:21) God's people treasure the book so how could they be in ignorance? Think about it. Do you ever neglect reading God's Word? Have you ever skipped reading more than one day? Thought so! II Kings 22 contains the story of King Josiah who gave instruction that God's house be repaired. When Hilkiah the priest went to count the money that had been collected for repairs years earlier, he was astonished to find "the book of the Law in the house of the Lord!" (v. 8) God's Law had been lost in the temple!

Throughout history evil rulers have tried to stamp out Christianity. During one of these times, a man hid his Bible above a door in a secret compartment. Because Christians gathered at his house regularly he was arrested. Officials could not find his Bible so they burned his house. His young daughter sneaked into the burning house and rescued the Bible. She wrapped it in her skirt and buried it in the garden. Friends later found Elsa lying in the garden, injured, but alive. This Bible was the only one left for many square miles.

Memorize that verse! Put it in your brain, no one can steal it.

Sleepy Morning

I feel so sleepy, so blah.
I do know what I should do,
But I want to take a nap
And disregard this cue.

Sweet sleep calls me so loudly.
My inner struggle is real.
Do I rise, take the high road,
or slump to what I feel?

I evaluate my plight:
Yes, last night my sleep was light.
"Go ahead and rest," I nod,
"Retired, I have a right!"

A sudden knock at the door
ends this battle in my head.
There'll be no nap for me. I
greet a smiling friend instead!

Alice Hein Schiel

(You're needed, wanted, pursued! You can do this!)

Hazel's Gem # 74:

"A fire kindled against an enemy often burns you more than him."

It's always best to let it go! My pastor Don White, told the story of how before he accepted Christ he was angry and determined to get even with someone. He hunted for the guy for twenty years. At that time Pastor Don worked for Southwestern Bell Telephone Company. He was all over Houston, Texas always watching and looking for the guy. When he finally found him he grabbed the guy and told him that he was gonna' get even with him. The guy looked at him and said, "What? I don't even know who you are." Pastor Don was in shock; here he was, walking in anger, dealing with developing ulcers and other health issues, spouting revenge and the "happy go lucky" guy didn't even remember the incident that started it all. Hatred binds YOU in its grip. The object of your hatred flies free. Pastor Don learned to "let it go."

Proverbs 26:27 (Amp) "Whoever digs a pit [for another man's feet] shall fall into it himself, and he who rolls a stone [up a height to do mischief] it will return upon him."

Romans 12:19 (Amp) "Beloved, never avenge yourselves, but leave the way open for [God's] wrath; for it is written, Vengeance is Mine, I will repay (requite) says the Lord."

Let God be your defense. Leave it to Him. It's so sweet!

Hazel's Gem # 75:
"Keep your tools sharp and God will find you work."

What a comforting thing to know. What are your tools? It could be your talents, your skills. It might be literal tools. The idea is to be ready.

I have seen it time and again: God provides work for you so you can earn money to meet your needs. Keep your focus on Him and don't let circumstances cloud your vision. The work may not always be what you'd prefer or your dream job, but if you prepare yourself, God will give you opportunity. Be ready and watch for the opportunity.

Proverbs 18:16 (Amp) "A man's gift makes room for him and brings him before great men."

If you want to be productive in God's kingdom – prepare! Pray, study the Bible (find a Bible, a Bible college), study music, speak, and sing. Opportunities await you today. Rehearse your testimony. Remind yourself of answered prayers. Be ready to encourage someone by sharing the story of your blessings.

Your gift will bring you before influential people. You will influence them or they will promote you. Be ready!

Hazel's Gem # 76:
"If your heart is aglow with the presence of God,
Its radiance will reach your face."

God's presence is like a warm fire on a wintry day or a cool breeze in summer's heat. God's presence is like a refreshing drink when you're very thirsty. It satisfies, it brings inner joy. God's presence brings confidence.

Psalms 92: 9 – 15 (Amp)

"For behold, Your adversaries, O Lord, for behold, Your enemies shall perish; all the evildoers shall be scattered.

"But my horn (emblem of excessive strength and stately grace) You have exalted like that of a wild ox; I am anointed with fresh oil.

"My eye looks upon those who lie in wait for me; my ears hear the evildoers that rise up against me.

"The [uncompromisingly] righteous shall flourish like the palm tree [be long-lived, stately, upright, useful, and fruitful]; they grow like a cedar in Lebanon [majestic, stable, durable, and incorruptible].

"Planted in the house of the Lord, they shall flourish in the courts of our God.

"[Growing in grace] they shall still bring forth fruit in old age; they shall be full of sap [of spiritual vitality] and [rich in the] verdure [of trust, love and contentment].

"[They are living memorials] to show that the Lord is upright and faithful to His promises; He is my rock, and there is no unrighteousness in Him."

How can one not smile? God's very presence is with YOU.

Alice Hein Schiel B.S., M.Ed.

Wait with hope

Hazel's Gem # 77:
"Patience is a virtue that carries a lot of **wait**!

No one wants to hear it: "Wait!" "Just wait and see!" We are so conditioned by fast speed internet, microwave ovens, and fast food restaurants that we sometimes devalue the virtue of patience.

Patience is not procrastination! Patience is enduring pain, trouble, with composure and without complaining. It is calmly tolerating insult, delay, and confusion. Christian friends are quick to warn you, "Don't pray for patience!" They see such a prayer as asking for trouble. The truth is that patience is a fruit which the Holy Spirit works in the life of the believer. (Galatians 5:22) If you follow Jesus Christ patience is growing in you and there are blessings attached to patience.

When Jesus gave instructions about the Holy Spirit coming he told believers to not depart from Jerusalem, but to "**wait** for the promise of the Father." (Acts 1:4) They put their lives on hold and waited. The Holy Spirit came in power with manifestations.

Isaiah 64:4 tells us that God acts on behalf of those who "**wait** for him."

Isaiah 40:31 "But they that **wait** upon the Lord shall renew their strength; they shall mount up with wings as eagles; they shall run, and not be weary; they shall walk, and not faint."

Wait with hope, with faith, the blessing is coming. You can sing and dance while you **wait**!

The myrtle blossoms!

"Pretty Girl"

Alice Hein Schiel

This morning two robins greet me
as I grope to find my way.
They bring such joy the shadows flee.
Light floods in to redeem my day!

Birds flit among myrtle blossoms;
they are singing now to me.
Above the chorus is the card'nal,
message delivered so joyfully!

"Pretty girl! Pretty girl!" he coos.
Daddy, laughing, points straight at me,
"Listen, girl! The bird sings to you!"
This mem'ry rises suddenly.

I smile and tuck it back inside.
Sweet bird continues with his song.
My smile increases, joy's a tide!
Melody echoes loud and long.

Just listen – now he sings to you!
"Pretty girl! Pretty girl!" Hear it?
The peace, the calm, life's fresh, all's new!
Wonderful song! That bird's got wit!

Always thrills me when I hear it.
Gotta' be a Number One Hit!

Hazel's Gem # 78:
"We need **not fear** the darkness of the world, for Christ the light is ever with us."

"**Let not** your heart be troubled: ye believe in God, believe also in me." John 14:1 (KJV). It's a command! You are in control. Do not allow yourself to be troubled. You have to trust that Jesus takes care of you. He has promised that he will never leave you (Matthew 28:20). So many scriptures command us to **Fear not**. It is our job to remind ourselves of this truth.

We can walk in Isaiah 43: 1, 2 because we are spiritual Israel. "But now thus saith the Lord that created thee, O Jacob, and he that formed thee, O Israel, **Fear not**: for I have redeemed thee, I have called thee by thy name; thou art mine. When thou passest through the waters, I will be with thee; and through the rivers, they shall not overflow thee: when thou walkest through the fire, thou shalt not be burned; neither shall the flame kindle upon thee."

Isaiah 41:13 "For I the Lord thy God will hold thy right hand, saying unto thee, **Fear not**; I will help thee."

Such powerful truth – God is with you, Jesus is with you, the Holy Spirit is in you! There is no place for fear.

Hazel's Gem #79:
"The **dewdrop** fulfills the Lord's will as much as the thunderstorm."

What a relief! You don't have to be the most impressive, the loudest, the best looking, the tallest, the smartest! All you have to do is fulfill your purpose. Be mindful that God is shining through you. Just perform your "job" today and do it well. Martin Luther King, Jr. admonished us to be the best at whatever we are when he stated, "If you are a street sweeper, be the best street sweeper!"

Just do your job well. Be who you are and make excellence your goal. You're gonna' have to mow the yard anyway. It may as well look good when you drive in the driveway! You're gonna' have to clean the kitchen so it may as well make you smile when you go in to make the coffee!

Think of it – even the greatest generals aren't winning battles every day of their lives. Some days they're learning, some days they're planning. If they do their job well, most days they're just enjoying peace.

….and the **dewdrops** bring moisture to the earth, the trees, the grass, the flowers. Relief from a dry, hot day is most welcome! **You** are refreshing!

"But now hath God set the members every one of them in the body, as it hath pleased him." I Corinthians 12:18

Alice Hein Schiel B.S., M.Ed.

Hazel's Gem # 80:
"The best way to keep happiness is to **give it away**."

It's as true as the law of gravity, perhaps more true.

Luke 6:38 "Give, and it shall be given unto you; good measure, pressed down, and shaken together, and running over, shall men give into your bosom. For with the same measure that ye mete withal it shall be measured to you again."

Ephesians 6:8 "Knowing that whatsoever good thing any man doeth, the same shall he receive of the Lord, whether he be bond or free."

Whether you are the employer or the employee, the parent or the child, the teacher or the student, this principle holds true. There's an old saying that declares, "He who brings sunshine into the lives of others cannot keep it from himself." A song admonishes us to "smile a while and give your face a rest."

Give happiness to others and you'll find yourself experiencing a deep satisfaction, happiness. Webster's dictionary says that if you are happy, you are favored by circumstances; you are lucky or fortunate. God's principle shows that you are favored when you spread happiness to others. Get started: buy a cup of coffee for someone, listen to the one who needs to talk, sweep someone's floor, babysit for a friend for a couple of hours (talk about giving)!

Hazel's Gem # 81:
> "I know not why His hand is laid in chastening on my life.
> Nor why today my little world is filled so full of strife
> But I do know that God is love, that He my burden shares
> And though I may not understand, I know for me He cares."

If you can only train yourself to accept correction quickly, the more quickly the correction will be done! God is going to correct you, so don't be upset!

Hebrews 12: 5&6 "...My son, despise not thou the chastening of the Lord, nor faint when thou art rebuked of him: For whom the Lord loveth he chasteneth, and scourgeth every son whom he receiveth."

Keep your thoughts balanced. Every trial you face is not chastening; but when it is, you'll know.

I love how the Amplified Bible explains it. "Whoever loves instruction and correction loves knowledge, but he who hates reproof is like a brute beast, stupid and indiscriminating." Prov. 12:1. Don't be stupid! Get yourself lined up with God's Word!

"He who refuses instruction and correction despises himself, but he who heeds reproof gets <u>understanding</u>." Prov. 15:32 (Amp). Proverbs 2:11 – 18 teaches that <u>understanding</u> brings long life, riches, honor, peace, and happiness.

"Poverty and shame come to him who refuses instruction and correction, but he who heeds reproof is honored." Prov. 13:18 (Amp)

Yep. Lining yourself up quickly is best!

Alice Hein Schiel B.S., M.Ed.

Message

There are words within me that must come out.
Will my writing be as loud as a shout?
The writing will last longer I do believe.
Today's inspiration must find its relief.

There are words within me that I must write.
I know the message will help bring sight
to those who simply cannot find their way,
to the successful starting another day.

I sit and ponder to get the words right.
I rearrange them in my head at night.
There's a truth that rises, pressing anew:
"I'm always writing by what I say and do."

This silent message rings out loud and clear.
What's my life breeding; is it faith or fear?
Am I spreading darkness or shedding light?
Daily lifesong's always rising, like a kite.

But still – there's words that burn inside of me!
I have to write them: "For life there's a Key!
Jesus is the message all hearts must believe!
His death and resurrection are the human soul's relief!

Alice Hein Schiel

Hazel's Gem # 82:
"If we're not as mature as we could be,
we're not as mature as we should be."

Oh, man! That hurts! The reality is that we never arrive, unless we die, of course. Life's journey is one where we are always growing, always changing, always stretching.

We are always learning to walk in love. We face new challenges daily. New people to get along with, new weirdos to work alongside of! (Don't be defensive. Bill says that everybody is weird to someone.)

In II Peter chapter one Peter explains that God has provided his word so we can escape the moral decay of the world. In verse 5 he tells us to develop **virtue** (excellence, Christian energy), in exercising virtue develop **knowledge**; verse 6 – in exercising knowledge develop **self-control,** in exercising self-control develop **stedfastness** (endurance), in exercising stedfastness develop **godliness;** verse 7 – in exercising godliness develop **brotherly affection**, in exercising brotherly affection develop **Christian love.** Verse 8 (Amplified Bible) "For as these qualities are yours and increasingly abound in you, they will keep (you) from being idle or unfruitful…"

That's a lot of exercising and developing! These qualities are yours. They abound in you more and more. Don't use your immaturity as an idle excuse, get busy exercising. Life is a long race. Enjoy today, but keep stretching.

Hazel's Gem # 83:
"If you don't want to taste the fruits of sin,
stay out of the devil's orchard."

It looks inviting! It brings pleasure for a short while, but the sinful fruit always grows.

Yesterday I was talking to a young man who is a recovered alcoholic. Nine years sober, he is looking healthy and feeling good. He said, "My old friends ask me what I do for fun these days and I say, 'Nothing.' The things I used to do 'for fun' were slowly chaining me and taking everything. That fun was stripping me: stealing my job, my family, my money, and my possessions. I woke up one day and admitted that I needed help. I asked God for help and I walked away from the destruction. I began a slow recovery. I went to rehab, then extended rehab, and I came out a new person. My life is fun! It's fun to be in control of my finances! It's fun to have a good job! It's fun to have a happy wife! I don't need the extreme! I take one day at a time."

Life is full of challenges no matter who you are. You will face mountains. Don't climb with the burden of sin's bricks on your back. You'll fall. Jesus said, "My yoke is easy and my burden is light." Matt. 11:30.

Hazel's Gem # 84:
"How you respond to temptation either makes you or breaks you."

"Blessed (happy to be envied) is the man who is patient under trial and stands up under temptation, for when he has stood the test and been approved, he will receive [the victor's] crown of life which God has promised to those who love Him." James 1:12 Amp

Train yourself to run away from sin. Seems like lately my temptations have involved relationships with people and being able to respond in a Christlike manner when I have been hurt. I Corinthians chapter 13 so pricks my heart. Verse one tells me that if I don't have love I am a noisy gong or a clanging cymbal. Verse 5 Amplified "Love is not conceited (arrogant and inflated with pride): it is not rude (unmannerly) and does not act unbecomingly. Love (God's love in us) does not insist on its own rights or its own way, for it is not touchy, or fretful or resentful; it takes not account of the evil done to it [it pays no attention to a suffered wrong]."

If your heart is having trouble catching up with what your head knows you must do, at least you can keep my mouth shut until you get your heart lined up! Prayer and the Holy Spirit bring clarity.

Hazel's Gem # 85:
"It takes unfair treatment to test the Christian's consecration."

Hazel's Gem # 86:
"Hem your blessings with praise lest they unravel."

It is always the right time to praise God! The hem of a garment is the bottom edge turned under and stitched to keep the garment from unraveling.

"He who offereth praise glorifieth Me; and to him that ordereth his conversation aright will I show the salvation of God." Psalms 50:23

One of my four teen-agers was extremely upset with me one day and ran into their bedroom, slamming and locking the door. I pounded and got no response so I unlocked the door. The window was open, screen hanging loose. I looked feverishly outside. My mind was racing, "So now I have a run-away?? I need to get to the bank with this deposit (we were business owners in those days). The bank closes in 30 minutes! I have to go. I don't know how to handle this anyway. I'll think while I drive."

As I drove I thought, "I really have no idea what to do!" So I began to pray and then I started singing praise to God. I sang all the way to the bank and all the way home. When I got home my teen was home, the bedroom window was closed, the chore we'd argued over was done! Neither one of us mentioned it again. Praise keeps blessings. Hem your day in praise!

Sounds of the Rain

Sounds of the Rain

Summer rain! Beauty and mystery!
Nature does sing in a jillion keys.

Pit! Pat! On my window pane.
Pit! Pat! I hear it again.

The Pit! Pat! Quickens as thunder roars.
Torrential downfall as creek levels soar.

One day, two days, three days, and still more?
The lovely Pit! Pat! Now beats the door.

Insects are buzzing their happy songs.
The frogs are croaking to sing along.

The water hums as it rushes by
drowning out the insects' lullaby.

Pink rain lilies stand at attention.
The bridges groan with their suspicion.

We think of rain and we think of life.
We think of floods and we think of strife.

Too much! Too much! The chickadees cry.
The whistler ducks leave; the pond's too high!

The turtles paddle to reach the edge.
The pedal boat totters on the ledge.

Four, five days! Won't it ever let up?
Pacing now like a whimpering pup.

A peaceful lull does cover the farm.
Raining has stopped; she has lost all charm.

Alice Hein Schiel B.S., M.Ed.

Sounds of the Rain
(cont'd)

We quickly dart out to look around.
Running water's a nerve-wracking sound.

Pasture's an ocean, my rain boot leaks.
I'm back inside as falling tree creaks.

My house is dry, but many are wet.
A sadness hoovers; don't let it sit!

Rain gauges drowned, covered park benches.
Places have had 50plus inches!

God's rainbow promise, resil'ant man;
Rescues galore, hearts driving the plans.

The sound of love is deafening now.
They're rescuing even the farmer's cow!

Loud TV tells the flood's full story:
Some old guy by the name of HARVEY.

(Hurricane Harvey flooded the Texas coast
in August of 2017.)

Alice Hein Schiel

(Hear God's voice even in the storm.)

Hazel's Gem # 87:
   "Christ sends none away empty,
   but those who are full of themselves."

Full of themselves, hmmmm. Conceited, proud, selfish, arrogant, and boastful are words that come to mind, the **Big I.** We all need to do a routine check-up from the neck up. Jesus, our Master, never made self number one. He always did the Father's will (John 17:4). As children we learned that true **JOY** is **J**esus, **O**thers, then **Y**ourself. It's good to remind yourself of that.

It's healthy to have a certain amount of self-confidence (actually, for the Christian: "I can do all things <u>through Christ</u>" Philippians 4:13), but balance is necessary. Without Christ, you are nothing.

"And those who belong to Christ Jesus (the Messiah) have crucified the flesh (the godless human nature) with its passions and appetites and desires."Gal. 5:24 Amp

Throughout Biblical history men and women who followed God have given of their time, wealth, and talents, selflessly. Nehemiah supported himself when he served as governor of the province of Judah. Queen Esther put her throne, even her life, on the line when she spoke up for the Jewish people.

In II Timothy 4:6 Paul said his life was about to be poured out as a drink offering. It's a delicate balance – you have to take care of the "self" God gave you, but you can't let "self" be the boss.

Hazel's Gem # 88:
"Unless we come apart and rest awhile,
we may just plain come apart."

When God organized life for His people, the Israelites, He set up a day of rest each week. Every seventh day the people were to **rest** from work and they were to **worship** God. They even had limits regarding how far they could travel on the Sabbath.

God designed our bodies. He knows how they work best. Rest allows our bodies to replenish.

Our lives can get pretty busy no matter what stage we're in. The responsibilities of raising children, the stresses of job, are thrilling adventures. We can't allow ourselves to get out of God's rhythm. A vacation time each year is not extravagant. A break from the routine of work, even a small break works wonders for your mind and body.

If you don't take time to rest you will wear yourself out more quickly than is necessary. These bodies won't last forever, but we can influence how efficiently we "run" and how healthy we are.

Jesus took time to come apart and pray. "Now in these days it occurred that He went up into a mountain to pray, and spent the whole night in prayer to God." Luke 6: 12. Prayer brings rest.

Hazel's Gem # 89:
"God is not looking for extraordinary men (women) for ordinary work, but ordinary men (women) for extraordinary work."

God is calling. There is never a reason to feel unqualified. Sure, the mission is demanding, but the boss is a miracle worker. He's better than Superman or Spiderman! He delights in using the weak.

"...not many mighty, not many noble, are called: But God hath chosen the foolish things of the world to confound the wise; and God hath chosen the weak things of the world to confound the things which are mighty." I Corinthians 1: 26b, 27

He has chosen ordinary people and used them for the extraordinary. **Nehemiah** who was a cupbearer to the king was used to rebuild the walls of Jerusalem while under attack warnings.

David, the shepherd boy, killed the giant that had Israel's armies paralyzed.

Daniel, a captive in a foreign country, survived the lions' den causing King Darius to declare Jehovah God the God of the land.

Mary, a common youth, became the mother of the King of the Universe!

God can use the talented and the untalented, the ordinary and the royal. He equips those He calls. He will make **you** everything you need to be for today's mission.

Hazel's Gem # 90:
>I looked at the mountain.
>"It is too hard, Lord. I cannot climb."
>"Take my hand," he whispered,
>"I will be your strength."
>
>I saw the road.
>"It is too long, Lord," I said, "so rough and long."
>"Take my love," he answered.
>"I will guard your feet."
>
>I looked at the sky.
>"The sun is gone," I said, "already it grows dark."
>"Take the lantern of my word," he whispered,
>"That will be light enough."

What a Savior! What a Lord! What a guide! What hope!

"The entrance and unfolding of Your words give light; their unfolding gives understanding (discernment and comprehension) to the simple."

Psalm 119:130 Amp

Walking with the King is invigorating because he sees the pitfalls, the danger; and He will guard you. Listen for His whisper. It could come through a friend, a child, or a preacher. If you can find a scripture to declare for the situation, the situation will change, or you will be changed. Don't be in a hurry to find resolution, wait for God's whisper. He is your strength. His light is enough.

Stretching

Alice Hein Schiel

The deepest love I've ever known
is from the Lord and Him alone.

The kindest hand I've ever felt:
His touch when I before him knelt.

He knows my motives, my mistakes;
sees that my heart is true, not fake.

He's close; when I whisper His name
He comes to guide me through the rain.

"Forgive me, Lord, when I can't see
the guiding light in front of me.

Forgive me, Lord, when I can't hear
obvious answers ringing clear (ly)

Getting back to knitty gritty!
There's no room for my self-pity!

The ones I love are just like me.
We're loving so imperfectly.

Help me to love the way You do –
patient, kind, protecting, and true.

The deepest love I've ever known
is from you, Lord, and you alone."

Hazel's Gem # 91:
"Sin causes the cup of joy to spring a leak."

One of the most amazing things about walking with God is the **joy** that you feel. Even as a child, when I decided to give my life to Jesus I experienced euphoria which bubbled up from inside of me! At church we sang the hymn "**Joy** Unspeakable". "It is joy unspeakable and full of–glory, full of – glory, full of – glory. It is joy unspeakable and full of glory! Oh the half has never yet been told!"

The church, all ages, would sing it out – the one who was freed from a life of much sin along with the youngest child – everyone felt the **joy** that Jesus brings. The song was based on I Peter 1:8 KJV: "Whom having not seen, ye love; in whom, though now ye see him not, yet believing, ye rejoice with **joy** unspeakable and full of glory:"

You know the **joy** I'm speaking of! For weeks after church camp or revival you were singing nonstop. But then, living life or dealing with humans, somehow anger came up or you made fun of someone, you lied (surely not, but maybe), you ignored your parents' rules – some sin caused the **joy** to leak out, bit by bit until you became stagnant. As an adult maybe your kids, spouse, or coworkers have provoked you. Walk away from that sin.

Psalms 45:7 KJV "Thou lovest righteousness and hatest wickedness: therefore God, thy God, hath anointed thee with the **oil of gladness** above thy fellows."

Hazel's Gem # 92:
> "I did it again today
> I guess I'm in a rut
> I missed an opportunity
> To keep my big mouth shut."

Tell it like it is! You have an opportunity to control your speech every day! For years communication has been the biggest problem in the church. Knowing when to speak up and when to keep quiet is one thing. Actually mastering the art is quite another. The apostle James who was pastor of the church in Jerusalem had much to say about it in chapter 3 of his book.

James 3:2 KJV "For in many things we offend all. It any man offend not in word, the same is a perfect man, and able also to bridle the whole body."

Verse 6 "…the tongue is a fire, a world of iniquity…it is set on fire of hell."

Verse 8 "But the tongue can no man tame; it is an unruly evil, full of deadly poison."

Feeling hopeless yet? You use this thing every day: your tongue! There has to be something positive. Think on it, we need this mouth to praise God, to encourage others!

Prov. 12:18 Amp "There are those who speak rashly, like the piercing of a sword, but the tongue of the wise brings healing!"

You knew what this meant before I started on it! Just let this be your reminder – you don't have to comment on everything!

Alice Hein Schiel B.S., M.Ed.

Hazel's Gem # 93:
"It's tragic to have a saved soul, but a wasted life."

How does someone waste their life? Could it be by not setting goals, by always taking the easy path? Perhaps it's by being a couch potato or a cell phone zombie. You could be wasting your life by letting addictions steal your health and wealth.

Each of us views waste through a different lens. A young entrepreneur may declare, "My time gaming was not wasted; I learned and developed a game that has brought me wealth."

Some want Christ as "fire insurance" only. They want to miss the eternal fires of hell, but don't want to be bothered otherwise. Others want to wait until they are old to get serious about serving God, wasting all their talents on selfish ideals.

God our father doesn't see any of us as "wasted." He treasures you much. In Luke 15:13 the younger son gathered all his portion "…and took his journey into a far country, and there **wasted** his substance with riotous living." Finally he returned to his father. In verse 20 "…But when he was a great way off, his father saw him, and had compassion, and ran, and fell on his neck, and kissed him."

The prodigal: safe, restored, and forgiven. Jesus is your path to the Father. Make your days count.

Hazel's Gem # 94:
"Despite inflation, the wages of sin remain unchanged."

It never gets any better. The wages of sin is always death. Sin will never benefit you. Any glitter or fun is a mirage, a lie. When sin finally pays off it's always the same – death.

Romans 3:23 KJV "All have sinned and come short of the glory of God;" We all have to deal with it.

Romans 6:23 KJV "For the wages of sin is death; but the gift of God is eternal life through Jesus Christ our Lord." Jesus' death has paid the price for your sin bringing life instead of death.

Romans 5:1 "Therefore being justified by faith, we have peace with God through our Lord Jesus Christ."

Get away from that sin. It's attractive, but cruel, hard, and deadly.

Receive God's gift! Smile! Life is available to you!

My Shepherd

Alice Hein Schiel

When I was but a kid, about nine,
I dreamed I saw the Savior divine.

Such presence, anointing encountered
My heart forever there indentured.

He was clothed in a long robe of white.
The entire scene was hallowed and bright.

Purest eyes commanded me to stare.
Lost was I in the love flowing there.

Those eyes kept looking straight toward me.
I struggle to describe it fully.

I feel their kindness, I hear them speak.
I know eyes don't speak, yet these eyes did,

"I am the **way**, I'm the **truth**, the **Life**."
Clearly spoken by those eyes of Christ.

I was entranced as time did linger.
Little ol' me with the **Great Shepherd**!

His hand did reach to touch my blonde head.
No fear, rushing joy I felt instead!

A dream or vision, I do not care.
He stole my heart, this Jesus there.

I awoke with a trembling heartbeat.
It just seemed so real, the warmth, the heat.

That night I sat in revival meet.
The minister said, "Stand to your feet."

"It's time to think, yes, it's time to pray.
You're invited to seek God today."

"You can feel God's touch and join God's team."
My heart softly whispered, "Like the dream!"

I hurried to pray, kneeling and such;
not disappointed, I felt that touch!

I've followed him fifty-plus years since,
never regretting pasture or fence.

What a shepherd he's been for this sheep!
He **captured** my heart, my soul he keeps.

Alice Hein Schiel B.S., M.Ed.

Hazel's Gem # 95:
> "When forming your opinions
> do it carefully – **go slow,**
> Hasty judgments oft are followed
> by regretting – that I know;
> And in arguments be careful not
> too quickly to decide –
> Try to look upon the subject
> from the other fellow's side – "

There's all kinds of wisdom here! It doesn't mean to have weak opinions, just informed ones. Think before you act. In debate class, having to debate for an opinion you despise will help you solidify your own opinion, or adjust it.

It even works well when training your children. Don't let them blind you, but be willing to listen before you pounce. Everyone has to make many, many split-second decisions daily. You move out of routine, experience, or habit. A simple mental count to ten before you engage can help bring clarity to your judgment so you can move purposely, caringly.

This quote is from the <u>Imitation of Christ</u> written in AD 1418 by Thomas a Kempis: "no one is sufficient for himself, no one is wise enough for himself; but we have to support one another, comfort one another, help, instruct, and admonish one another." (Book I, chapter 16)

Proverbs 21:23 KJV "Whoso keepeth his mouth and his tongue keepeth his soul from troubles."

Go slow. (not drive slow, go slow)

Hazel's Gem # 96:
"If you are unkind, you're the wrong kind."

Meanness doesn't work in the kingdom. Rudeness is unacceptable. All the cute "put downs" are not cute to Father God.

This is a day for kindness. It's popular with our Heavenly Father. You can't overdo it.

Try being kind to your boss or your spouse. They'll think you're up to something.

Ephesians 4:32 "And be ye **kind** one to another, tender-hearted, forgiving one another, even as God for Christ's sake hath forgiven you."

If you are Christ's, kindness grows in you. The strong, "table turning," "devil defeating," "storm stopping," "walking for miles" Jesus was kind. You should be too.

Hazel's Gem # 97:
"Gossip is like soft soap – mostly **lye**!"

Not the tongue again! She's relentless. I wonder why Hazel recorded so many gems about our words. Hmmmm.

Lye is a strong alkaline solution obtained by leaching wood ashes and it can be used for cleaning or in making soap. To **lie** is to make statements one knows to be false. Gossip can be malicious truth or lie. I remember the "gossip game" from my teen-age years. We would sit in a circle and one person would cup their hand and whisper something in the ear of the one on their right. No one else could hear the message. The second person would whisper it to the third, etc. As the message progressed wide eyes, facial expressions, and giggles would begin to give one the hint, "They didn't hear what I heard!" The last person to get the message would say it aloud. Everyone roared with laughter because of how the message had changed. Be careful when repeating things – your audience may be hard of hearing, or have selective hearing.

Don't feel bad. Peter also kept reminding believers to get it right.

I Peter 1:13 Amp "I think it right, as long as I am in this tabernacle (tent, body), to stir you up by way of remembrance."

So remember: **you** can do this! No gossip!

Hazel's Gem # 98:
"Too many people make cemeteries of their lives by burying their **talents**."

Come on! Get your shovel! Dig them up! Only you know the talents you have buried.

I've heard a quote that goes something like this: "My life is God's gift to me; what I do with my life is my gift to Him."

"But I didn't receive the best talent or the most talents." So what?

In Matthew chapter 25 Jesus told a story about a servant who hid his **talent** (in this case, about $1,000 entrusted to him by his master) in the earth because he was afraid. Two other servants had been given more. When the master returned he dug up the talent to give it back. The master was very angry and told him that if he didn't want to use the talent, he should at least have put it in the bank to draw interest. Verse 30a (Amp) "And throw the good-for-nothing servant into the outer darkness."

Use what God has given you. Get some training, hang around talented people, buy yourself some supplies or seeds, or whatever!

President John F. Kennedy got his staff's attention when he said, "I think this is the most extraordinary collection of **talent**, of human knowledge, that has ever been gathered at the White House – with the possible exception of when Thomas Jefferson dined alone."

You may or may not be a Thomas Jefferson; just **use** the **talents you** have!

Alice Hein Schiel B.S., M.Ed.

I Can't Live in the Valley

I am running through this valley.
I can feel the stress surround me, Lord.
I know that this is not your place for me.
I'm so sick and tired of cryin', Lord.
Can't change what others have done, O Lord.
I think that I'll just cast these cares on you!

I can't live in the valley,
Can't live in the valley.
I've been on the mountain with Jesus too long!

I can't stay in the valley,
Can't stay in the valley.
My place is on the mountain top with him!

To get out of this valley
I am leaping over problems, Lord.
Bad attitudes I'm leaving down below.
I'm casting down the negatives,
I'm holding to your promises.
My faith is in the shepherd of my soul.

I can't live in the valley,
Can't live in the valley.
I've been on the mountain with Jesus too long!

I can't stay in the valley,
Can't stay in the valley.
My place is on the mountain top with him!

(a song I wrote, dealing with disappointments, moving forward)

Alice Hein Schiel

Hazel's Gem # 99:
> "I thank you for my problems, Lord,
> And every trying strife
> For each one that you solve for me
> Puts new **joy** in my life."

Walking with the King of Kings and Lord of Lords is always an adventure. When the path is rough he will steady you. If there are roadblocks, there is a path somewhere and he will show it to you if you will pay attention to him and listen.

Life is like endurance training: each trial you master, you get stronger. The next time, even though the trial may be harder, it's easier to trust, easier to focus on the light at the end. You're becoming a stronger person on the inside. Your spiritual muscles are growing. You can handle everything that comes if you let God strengthen you.

James 1:2-4
"My brethren, count it all **joy** when ye fall into divers temptations;

"Knowing this, that the trying of your faith worketh patience.

"But let patience have her perfect work, that ye may be perfect and entire, wanting nothing."

Whatever you will face this day it will lead to joy if you let God work in the situation. Ask him to be your guide. See the trial as a stepping stone or a spiritual exercise. You've got this!

Hazel's Gem # 100:
"The measure of a truly great man is the courtesy with which he treats the little man."

When Jesus' disciples began to discuss who among them would be the greatest, he sat down and instructed them. "If any man desire to be first, the same shall be last of all, and servant of all." Mark 9:35b

Jesus told the parable of the Pharisee (religious man), and the publican in Luke chapter 18. Verse 9 says that he told it to those "which despised others."

There were many publicans in Judea at the time of Christ. To Jews, being a publican (tax collector for Rome) was an odious thing. In this parable the Pharisee looks to heaven and prays thanking God that he is not "even as this publican. I fast twice in the week, I give tithes of all that I possess." The publican would not look up, but asked God for mercy. Jesus concludes in verse 14, this publican was "justified rather than the other: for everyone that exalteth himself shall be abased; and he that humbleth himself shall be exalted."

Paul reemphasizes it, "...but in lowliness of mind let each esteem other better than themselves." Philippians 2:3b

It's not a fake humility or a poor self-image; it's clearly seeing that we are all "the best of God's creation" in His eyes. Appreciate his "human creatures" today.

Maturing

You see things in others that
you wish you could display.
You notice their saintly qualities and cringe.

"Let me be more like Tinka
who encourages, lifts up,
uses her influence to promote others."

"Let me be more like Mr. Earl
who helps the widows; and
uses humor to punctuate his teachings."

"Let me be more like Bill
who makes wise judgments and
always seems to sense people's stellar motives."

"Let me be more like Debbie.
She's got it together!
She's cool, collected, smiling, always on time."

You can show good qualities!
You can be more, much more!
It's your time to put down roots and start growing!

What are you feeding yourself?
Fertilize the virtues.
Water your life with the good influences.

Who you are today is the
result of what you processed yesterday.
Keep pressing toward the goal!

Hazel's Diamond (repeated):
"Today's mighty oak is just yesterday's little
nut that held its ground."

Alice Hein Schiel B.S., M.Ed.

Scriptures Used

Gem # 1	Psalms 121: 1, 2, 5-7
Gem # 4	Matthew 7: 1-3
Gem # 5	Psalms 138: 3, 7
Gem # 6	Psalms 91: 11-13
Gem # 7, 8	Romans 12: 19b, 21
Gem # 9	Galatians 5: 21, 22, 23
Gem # 10	Genesis 12: 2 Amplified Bible
Gem # 11	Luke 11: 10
Gem # 12, 13	I Corinthians 13:1
Gem # 14	Psalms 121: 1, 2a
Gem # 15, 16	Psalms 19, 14
Gem # 17	II Cor. 3:2 Amplified Bible
Gem # 18	Psalms 23: 6
Gem # 19, 20, 21	Hebrews 10: 25a
Gem # 22	Psalms 103: 1-5
Gem # 23, 24, 25	Matthew 6: 14, 15
Gem # 26, 27	Proverbs 17: 22
Gem # 28	Psalms 119: 105; Mark 10: 44, 45
Gem # 29, 30	James 1:19; 3:2; 3:6
Gem # 31	I Thess. 5: 18
Gem # 32	I Peter 2:17; II Tim. 1:7
Gem # 33	Matthew 10: 29, 31
Gem # 34, 35	II Corinthians 6: 18
Gem # 36	Psalms 8: 3-6
Gem # 37, 38	Psalms 23: 4, 5

Gem # 39, 40	Matthew 7: 3-5
Gem # 41	Galatians 2: 20a
Gem # 42	Rom. 10: 9; Eph. 2:19, 4:12
Gem # 43	Prov. 15: 15b; Neh. 8: 10
Gem # 44	I Peter 1:25; II Tim. 3:16, 17; II Peter 1:20, 21
Gem # 45	I Kings 19: 11, 12
Gem # 46	Rom. 12: 11 Amplified Bible
Gem # 47	Prov. 15: 32a; Rev. 3: 19 Amplified Bible
Gem # 48	Matthew 6: 19, 20
Gem # 49	Romans 12:3c
Gem # 50	Luke 19: 8
Gem # 51	I Corinthians 5: 52
Gem # 52	Philippians 4: 11
Gem # 53	John 4: 24
Gem # 54	Isaiah 61: 3
Gem # 55	Romans 10:9; I John 1: 9
Gem # 56	Eccl. 9: 10a Amplified Bible
Gem # 57	Matthew 5: 14-16
Gem # 58	II Chronicles 16: 9a
Gem # 59	I Cor. 13: 7 Amplified Bible; James 5: 16a Amplified Bible
Gem # 60	Luke 20: 17b, 18; Ezekiel 36: 26; Luke 4: 18a
Gem # 61	I Thess. 5:17; Romans 14:12
Gem # 62	Deut. 28: 6, 7, 13; Ezekiel 20: 12
Gem # 63	Proverbs 25: 28, 16: 32
Gem # 64	I Peter 1: 24; Matt. 22: 37-39
Gem # 65	Phil. 4:13; Psalms 119:47 Amplified Bible; I Thess. 5:11; I Thess. 5:23 Amplified Bible
Gem # 66	II Cor. 4:18 Amplified Bible; Lam. 3:22, 23a Amplified Bible
Gem # 67	Matthew 5: 13
Gem # 68	Prov. 18: 24b; Psms. 27:10, 103:5, 119:103; John 4: 32; Malachi 3: 10-12
Gem # 69	I Cor. 13: 4
Gem # 70	I John 4: 4
Gem # 71	Matt. 13: 44; Psalms 19: 10b

Gem # 72	Psalms 20:7; III John 2
Gem # 73	II Peter 1: 21; II Kings 22: 8
Gem # 74	Prov. 26:27 Amplified Bible; Rom. 12:19 Amplified Bible
Gem # 75	Proverbs 18: 16 Amplified Bible
Gem # 76	Psalms 92:9-15 Amplified Bible
Gem # 77	Gal. 5:22; Acts 1:4; Isaiah 64:4, 40:31
Gem # 78	John 14:1; Matt. 28:20; Isaiah 43: 1,2, 41: 13
Gem # 79	I Corinthians 12: 18
Gem # 80	Luke 6:38; Ephesians 6: 8
Gem # 81	Hebrews 12: 5,6; Prov. 12:1; Prov. 15:32 Amplified Bible, Prov. 13:18 Amplified Bible; refers to Prov. 2:11-18
Gem # 82	II Peter 1: 5-8 Amplified Bible
Gem # 83	Matthew 11: 30
Gem # 84, 85	James 1:12 Amplified Bible; I Cor. 13: 1, 5 Amplified Bible
Gem # 86	Psalms 50:23
Gem # 87	John 17:4; Phil. 4:13; Gal. 5:24 Amplified Bible; II Tim. 4:6
Gem # 88	Luke 6: 12
Gem # 89	I Corinthians 1: 26b, 27
Gem # 90	Psalms 119:130 Amplified Bible
Gem # 91	I Peter 1: 8; Psalms 45: 7
Gem # 92	James 3: 2, 6, 8; Prov. 12: 18 Amplified Bible
Gem # 93	Luke 15: 13, 20
Gem # 94	Romans 3:23, 6:23, 5:1
Gem # 95	Proverbs 21: 23
Gem # 96	Ephesians 4: 32
Gem # 97	I Peter 1: 13 Amplified Bible
Gem # 98	Matt. 25: 30a Amplified bible
Gem # 99	James 1: 2-4
Gem # 100	Mark 9:35b; Luke 18:9, 14; Phil. 2:3b

That's a lot of WORD you took in. Keep it going!

Dear Reader,

I hope your spirit has been lifted and that your walk with God has been enriched by reading this book. As we walk with Christ we come to realize that our main purpose in life is "reconciliation." We are God's ministers of reconciliation. I have enjoyed writing these messages bringing Him near to you.

Thank you for your support. I'd love to hear from you if you would like to write. I will get back to you, and that may take a bit depending on schedules, life, etc. But I will do my best to get back with you.

Blessings,

Alice Hein Schiel
schielbunch@att.net is my email address

My first book ***Nora Mae, a Remarkable, Insignificant Person*** is available at Xulonpress.com, barnesandnoble.com, and amazon.com. (Any bookstore can order it for you. It is available through Ingram Book Company and/or Spring Arbor Book Distributors.)

Nora Mae, a Remarkable, Insignificant Person was a winner in the **John Weaver Excellent Reads Award** for **Non-fiction: Biography.** The book is the moving story of a woman in small town Somerville, Burleson County, Texas. The reader feels Nora's rejection, her fortitude, her creativity, and then her faith and driving compassion as she ages. It is a story that moves the reader from anticipation to sadness to joy, with a constant underlying sense of hope.

CPSIA information can be obtained
at www.ICGtesting.com
Printed in the USA
BVHW082034250219
541129BV00010B/87/P